ILLUSTRATED
LIBRARY
OF
WONDERS.
SCRIBNER, ARMSTRONG, & CO., NEW YORK

Fig. 28.—First wash of the Diamond-yielding Soil in Brazil.

DIAMONDS

AND

PRECIOUS STONES,

A POPULAR ACCOUNT OF GEMS.

CONTAINING

THEIR HISTORY, THEIR DISTINCTIVE PROPERTIES, AND A DESCRIPTION OF THE MOST FAMOUS GEMS; GEM CUTTING AND ENGRAVING, AND THE ARTIFICIAL PRODUCTION OF REAL AND OF COUNTERFEIT GEMS.

TRANSLATED FROM THE FRENCH OF

LOUIS DIEULAFAIT,
Professor of Physics, Doctor of Sciences.

BY FANCHON SANFORD.

ILLUSTRATED BY 126 ENGRAVINGS ON WOOD.

NEW YORK:
SCRIBNER, ARMSTRONG, AND COMPANY.
1876.

RIVERSIDE, CAMBRIDGE:
STEREOTYPED AND PRINTED BY
H. O. HOUGHTON AND COMPANY.

PREFACE.

It would be easy for any one who had sufficiently prepared himself by previous study to write a purely scientific work on the subject of precious stones; but this is not the intention of the present writer, who aims at interesting a wider class of readers than a work of the kind indicated would reach.

In addition to the strictly scientific information to be given regarding precious stones, there are connected with them a great many facts not less interesting, and equally important for the public to know. To these we have devoted several sections of the following work.

In our times precious stones are used almost exclusively for the purpose of ornament, but in former times the case was very different. By reference to the authors of antiquity, as well as to those of the middle ages and the Renaissance, we have shown the important part that they then played, and what ideas prevailed regarding them.

From the thousands of fables and superstitions of which precious stones have been the subject, we have selected a certain number. In doing so we have disregarded those calculated only to interest the curious, and have chosen such as were likely to instruct and enlighten.

In Parts iv. and v. it was necessary to introduce some of the elements of crystallography, without which those two important chapters would have lost a great part of their value. We have treated the subject, however, as briefly as possible, but, at the same time, in a strictly scientific manner. To attempt to popularize science, by stripping it, as is so often done, of that which constitutes its very essence, is not to popularize, but to disfigure and travesty it.

The part devoted to counterfeit precious stones will not be one of the least useful. The facts which it contains will carry their own teaching with them, and of this the purchasers of precious stones will know how to avail themselves.

In another part the methods are explained, by means of which modern savants have succeeded in producing the majority of the precious stones. These methods, and the remarkable results obtained by the employment of them, have hitherto remained locked up in collections of scientific papers, or in special treatises. We are glad to have had the opportunity of first making them known to the public at large.

The illustrations interspersed through the book all reproduce as accurately as possible by engraving the objects they profess to represent, and none of them are fancy sketches. The utmost care has been bestowed on this department; for, if the engraver's art is one of the most powerful means of spreading knowledge, it can only be so by the exact reproduction of nature.

Lastly, we have constantly endeavoured to arrange facts according to their natural relations, so as, by the mere exposition, to exhibit, in a succinct form, a notable stage in the development of the human mind, both from an intellectual and a scientific point of view.

LOUIS DIEULAFAIT.

CONTENTS.

PART I.

PART II.

PART III.

PART IV.

PART V.

LIST OF THE ILLUSTRATIONS.

DIAMONDS

AND

PRECIOUS STONES.

PART I.

Precious Stones: their Origin; Geological Position; Physical Characteristics; Optical and Electrical Properties; External Characteristics; Susceptibility to the action of Light and Heat.

> "The jewel that we see, we stoop and raise;
> But that we do not see, we tread upon,
> And never think of it."

In the following pages we intend to treat not merely of precious stones strictly so called—that is, such mineral substances as have in all times attracted the attention of man by their hardness, their brilliancy, their colour, their scarcity, &c., but also of a certain number of productions which have nothing in common with the true precious stones, either in composition or origin, but which as articles of finery and adornment play precisely the same part as the latter.

When we contemplate the boundless wealth of nature we might imagine that the number of precious stones would be unlimited; but this, as we shall see, is far from being the case. We must remark, however, that it is impossible to draw a hard and fast line between the most common *precious* stones and *ordinary* stones, since we have here a particular case of the grand law formulated more than a century ago by the illustrious Linnæus: *Natura non facit saltus*—"Nature never makes a leap."

ORIGIN OF PRECIOUS STONES.

All precious stones are transparent, or at least translucent, from which it may be concluded that the matter of which each consists is homogeneous. Now this homogeneity could never have been attained by the mixture of their elements in the solid state, however finely these may have been pulverized, and hence they must have been in the condition of either gases or liquids. Nature has a multitude of means by which these transformations of matter are effected, all referable to three general processes:—

1st. Direct fusion of the substance by the action solely of heat.

2d. Dissolution of the substance by the aid of foreign substances at variable temperatures.

3d. Bringing together, in the state of vapours, substances destined to become the elements of the stone.

Fig. 1.—Igneous Rocks; the Volcano of Jorullo, in Mexico.

From the point of view of their formation, therefore, precious stones may be naturally divided into two classes.

The first comprehends stones produced by direct fusion, by crystallization in an excess of their melted substance, by volatilization of their elements; in a word, *by the direct intervention of heat.*

The second includes stones which have been formed in the midst of a solution of which *water* has been generally one of the constituent elements.

Hence some precious stones are met with in those portions of our globe which have been subjected to a high temperature, while others are found in those that have never supported such a temperature, or what comes to the same thing, that have been perfectly cooled at the period when they furnished to the water the elements of the stones of which we are speaking.

It is therefore of some importance to distinguish those portions of our globe which have been subjected to the action of fire from those that have not; and this is easily done.

GEOLOGICAL POSITION.

When we consider the solid part of our globe we recognize immediately its division into *earth*,—using that word in its agricultural sense; and *stones*

—more or less detached, or in the state of continuous rocks. The least examination shows further, that this earth itself is composed to a great extent of stones gradually decreasing in size; so that we easily arrive at the well-established conclusion that the earth and the stones have the same origin.

If then, in thought, we remove from the surface of the land the earth, whose thickness indeed is very inconsiderable, we perceive that the solid part of our globe consists exclusively of rocks.

These rocks are divided into two great classes: one formed of melted materials, like the lavas of our modern volcanoes; the other produced by seas, rivers, and lakes of ancient periods, in the same manner as we see deposits accumulated by the waters in our own time. The first are called *igneous* rocks; the second, *sedimentary.*

The Igneous Rocks, pushed from the interior of the earth in a plastic state, lift themselves above the surface of the soil in irregular shapes, in precipitous peaks, or vast cones, and sometimes in those basaltic columns whose aspect is so striking and impressive.

The accompanying cut exhibits a good example of these basaltic rocks, but we may remark that columnar basalt is comparatively rare, and that igneous rocks in general possess no regularity of structure. Very frequently they are intersected by cracks in all directions—a feature produced by the contraction resulting froom cooling.

The Sedimentary Rocks present an aspect so

Fig. 2.—Horizontal Columnar Basalt at St. Helena.

completely different from that of igneous formations, that they may be recognized at a great distance, even by inexperienced eyes. Being deposited in water in parallel layers, they have preserved the same disposition after being left dry. Sometimes, indeed, the horizontal layers have been singularly displaced from their original direction: sudden changes and movements of the soil have tilted them up and contorted them; but still the parallelism of the strata, and their disposition by successive layers, is nearly always clearly discernible. Fig. 3 is an

Fig. 3.—Structure of Sedimentary Rocks.

example of sedimentary rock, and it shows very distinctly the regularity of structure which these rocks usually display.

Beyond this general distinction there is another,

less prominent perhaps, but quite as definitely marked. The remains of myriads of animals and

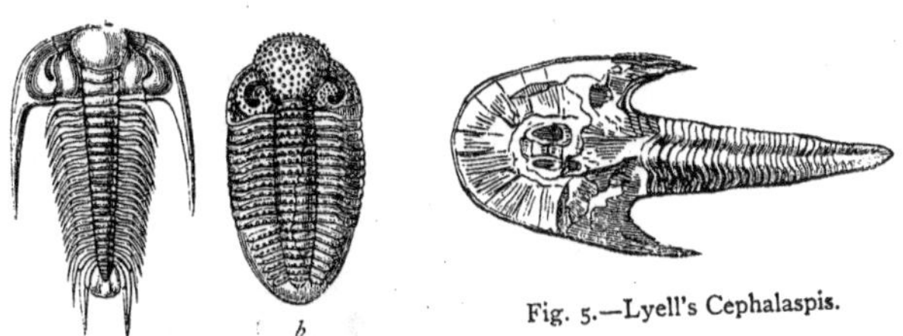

Fig. 5.—Lyell's Cephalaspis.

Fig. 4.—Trilobites.
a, Paradoxides bohemicus. *b*, Phacops latifrons.

plants have been left age after age in the sediments of the different eras; these remains are known as Fossils. They reveal forms of life very different

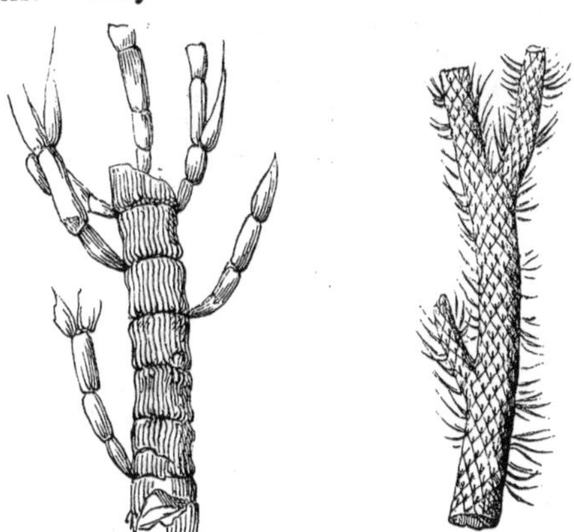

Fig. 6.—Calamite. Fig. 6ª.—Lepidodendron of the Coal Formation.

from those that exist in the present condition of our globe; and their dominant races, long since extinct, have furnished names for remote eras,—for all the geological ages, indeed, included between the azoic age and the age of man.

With the high temperature of the igneous formations, life was incompatible; consequently no fossil

Fig. 7.—Fossil Dragon-fly of the Secondary Epoch.

ever appears, or possibly could appear, in rocks of this kind. In sedimentary formations, on the contrary, such remains abound, and furnish another excellent means of distinguishing them from the igneous rocks.

A few illustrations will exemplify types of animal and vegetable fossils incident to different periods.

Figs. 4, 5, and 6 represent animal and vegetable forms that existed in a period incalculably remote,

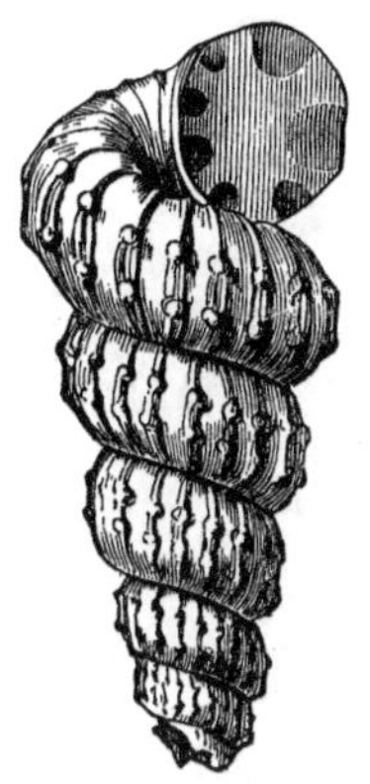

Fig. 8.—Turrilites catenata.

Fig. 9.—Terebratula.

Fig. 10.—Mammillary Ammonite.

and are found in rocks belonging to what has been called the primary or palæozoic period.

Those represented by Figs. 7, 8, 9, and 10 appertain to the secondary formations, such as the oolite or jurassic formation, named from the Jura Mountains, in whose rocks such specimens are

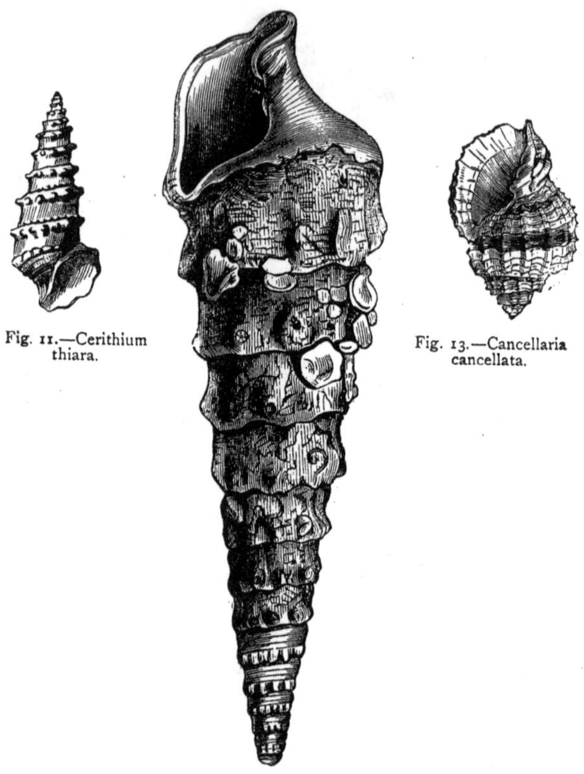

Fig. 11.—Cerithium thiara.

Fig. 12.—Gigantic Cerithium.

Fig. 13.—Cancellaria cancellata.

found; and the cretaceous period, or period of the chalk, next in order of time.

To the cretaceous period succeeded the tertiary

formation, in which are found such shells as those represented by Figs. 11, 12, and 13. By this time creatures had begun to appear bearing a strong

Fig. 14.—The Great Palæotherium.

resemblance to those of the present period. Figs. 14 and 15 illustrate characteristic types.

After the tertiary formation comes the post-tertiary or quarternary formation, in which the animals are quite analogous to those of our own period.

If we inquire of chemistry what is the composition of the two grand classes of rocks above-mentioned, we obtain this simple answer:—The calcareous element predominates in all sedimentary formations (excepting the most ancient); silicious and aluminous elements in igneous formations.

Fig. 15.—The Common Anoplotherium.

Consequently, *stratification*, *presence* and often extreme abundance of fossils, great *preponderance* of *the calcareous element*, are the unmistakable characteristics of sedimentary formations. *Absence* of *stratification*, complete *absence* of *fossils*, great preponderance of the silicious and aluminous elements, are the characteristics of igneous formations.

Now if we investigate the chemical composition of precious stones, we shall find that the greater number of those which really merit this appellation, are principally formed of silica and alumina, or of one of these two substances. It follows, then, that precious stones should be found most frequently in igneous formations, or in the débris of such formations: and we naturally conclude that they will be most abundant in countries where the geological development is chiefly of this kind. Theoretically this is true; but practically the *finding* of precious stones depends far more upon the condition than upon the abundance of the igneous rocks. These eagerly sought treasures are only the very rare exceptions in enormous masses of rock, and the latter must be broken up into small fragments before their riches can appear.

We know that under the influence of atmospheric agencies the most obdurate rock is gradually disintegrated; but atmospheric action has feebly contributed to the production of sands and the formation of arable lands. In different periods of its existence our globe has experienced agitations of extreme violence, the principal effects of which, after the lapse of countless centuries, are at this day perfectly discernible.

The last of these grand commotions belongs to the period which geologists have named the quarternary, an epoch relatively not far removed from our own.

Floods of water at that time spread across the

continents; mountains of ice, of which the Alpine glaciers are but meagre vestiges, invaded even the most temperate zones; streams of irresistible violence —such as the great rivers of our day can scarcely give us any idea of—furrowed the earth. Under the influence of these agencies, the stupendous forces of which were all working in one direction, the grinding down and destruction of the rocks was effected over vast spaces, and to considerable depths. Now it is precisely in the débris of igneous rocks, whose reduction to sand was accomplished during this period, that the greater number of precious stones are found; and above all, the diamond.

But although the diamond-producing soils are comparatively modern alluvial formations, it must not be concluded that the diamond, and the other precious stones which accompany it, are of recent origin. In reality, that which is recent is the reduction of the rocks to the alluvial state; but the rocks themselves, and consequently the precious stones that they contain, are often extremely ancient. There are precious stones whose existence was anterior to the first sedimentary formations; they had their place in the world long before the plants and animals began their measureless succession; and they are an inheritance to man from the azoic age, when as yet no foreshadowing of his existence had fallen upon the globe.

PHYSICAL CHARACTERISTICS OF PRECIOUS STONES.

WEIGHT AND MOLECULAR ACTION.

Specific gravity.—Every one knows that two equal volumes of different substances have seldom the same weight: a piece of lead, for instance, is much heavier than a piece of wood exactly equal to it in size. If we find the weight of a substance, and also that of an equal volume of another substance, *selected as a term of comparison* (distilled water is the term that has been chosen), and if we divide the weight of the first body by that of the second, we obtain a number which expresses how many times, and fractions of times, the body considered is more or less heavy than that to which it is compared. The number thus obtained is its *specific gravity.*

In the case of precious stones it is a characteristic of extreme importance, for it is frequently the means by which the difference is detected between stones that the eye might easily confound. In this way, for example, the diamond can be at once distinguished from the zircon, the specific gravity of the former being 3·4, and that of the latter 4·4.

Hardness.—We should be careful not to fall into the very frequent error of confounding the quality of hardness with that of resistance to crushing or concussion. There are minerals that may be crumbled between the fingers, and that are yet none the less hard. The hardness of a substance, according to the definition of Delafosse, is "the resistance which it opposes to the action of a point like that of a steel needle which may be drawn across it, or to the angular part of another mineral passed with friction over its surface."

Hardness is an indispensable quality of gems. If a stone were not very hard, the continual friction to which it is subjected would very soon destroy its polish; and with the polish, transparency, brilliancy, fire—all that constitutes its value—would vanish.

It is owing to this quality of hardness, added to the unchangable nature of their substance, that stones, cut perfectly by Egyptian artists thousands of years ago, have reached us intact; and give us the most interesting proof of the progress in arts and civilization which had been attained in those remote periods.

Fusibility.—Fusibility is the property which solid bodies possess of passing into the liquid state, when they are subjected to a sufficient temperature.

For precious stones in particular the point of fusion is lower in proportion as the composition of the stone is more complex. Thus the diamond, *a simple body*, is absolutely infusible. The ruby, the sapphire, the topaz, *binary bodies*, can only be melted before the oxyhydrogen blowpipe. The simple silicates, *ternary bodies*, are fusible at a much lower temperature; and the multiple silicates offer no serious resistance.

The temperature of fusion of precious stones, since it is allied in a remarkable manner with their hardness, serves as a good characteristic for distinguishing them.

OPTICAL PROPERTIES.

Refraction.—When a luminous ray passes through a homogeneous medium, its course is in a straight line, as shown in Fig. 16, a phenomenon with which everyone is familiar. But when it passes from one medium into another, the case is generally different, and the ray suffers a remarkable modification. It is then more or less diverted from its primitive direction, and has the appearance of being *broken*, whence the phenomenon has been termed *refraction*. A stick plunged into water will exemplify this effect.

The extent to which the luminous rays are diverted in traversing transparent bodies varies greatly. This variation is generally connected with differences in the nature and composition of the refracting bodies; but it is likewise intimately connected, as experiments prove, with the molecular constitution of these bodies. For example, Iceland spar and aragonite, whose chemical composition is identical, both consisting of pure carbonate of lime, refract the light unequally, for the sole reason that their *molecular constitution* is very different.

Fig. 16.—Course of a luminous ray in a homogeneous medium.

Double Refraction.—Among diaphanous bodies there is a numerous class of substances that possess the curious quality of presenting two images of one object. If a crystal of Iceland spar is placed upon a piece of white paper bearing an inscription, as in Fig. 17, two images will be visible of every point, and both images will show deviation. This is an instance of what is called *double refraction.*

When a body, crystallized or not, is perfectly homogeneous in all its parts, so that its elements are disposed everywhere in a uniform manner, one can easily understand that the light must traverse it regularly, and must present a single image of every object: such bodies possess the property of *simple refraction.*

Fig. 17.—Double refraction of Iceland spar.

Crystals belonging to the monometric or tesseral system, as the cube or octahedron, since their molecular disposition is perfectly regular, never exhibit the phenomenon of double refraction, in whatever direction they are traversed by the light; but crystals of all other systems possess the power of *double refraction*, differing in its effects as the crystal appertains to a system more or less closely related to the regular system.

As all precious stones that are highly valued are

crystallized, and it has been well ascertained what stones display *simple* and what stones *double* refraction, it sometimes becomes a matter of importance to know whether a given stone is really doubly-refrangent, in order to distinguish it from one which possesses simple refraction, but to which in other respects it is quite similar in appearance. As precious stones are all small, a special method of procedure is here necessary in order to obtain the phenomenon of double refraction.

Take, for example, a small stone, cut in form of a brilliant, concerning whose nature there is some doubt.

Place the stone at a level with the eye, holding it in one hand; in the other hand take an object of small dimensions, a pin for instance, and move it slowly on the other side of the stone until the eye is able to perceive it. If the stone is doubly-refractive, the rays will bifurcate on entering it, and accordingly two images of the pin will be seen, if it is not held too near the stone. If it is held very near the stone, the rays will not be far enough apart at the point where they emerge into the air to allow their separation to be evident.

If the experiment is made at night, instead of a pin a lighted candle may be used, the candle being placed beyond the reach of currents of air, so that its flame may be pure and regular. The phenomenon will be exactly the same, and have the aspect presented by Fig. 18.

If the phenomenon of double refraction is produced, the conclusion may be made without hesitation that the stone tested is not a diamond; for the diamond, since it appertains to the cubic (monometric) system, possesses simple refraction. The stone experimented on, therefore, is no doubt one of those with which the diamond is sometimes confounded, such as the sapphire and the zircon, which possess double refraction.

Fig. 18.—Aspect of a candle seen through a doubly-refractive crystal.

Polarization.—It is well known that if a beam of light falls upon a plane and polished surface it is reflected; but it is not so well known that if to this ray, which has already been reflected at a certain angle, a second mirror with plane inclined is presented, there are certain positions in which the ray will be no longer reflected by the second mirror. The light has acquired by its first reflection a profound modification, which is designated by the name of *polarization by reflection.*

In traversing certain crystals the light is subjected to the same changes; that is to say, the rays emerging from the crystal are no longer reflected when they fall at a certain angle upon a plane mirror; and they have become completely powerless to traverse certain crystals, otherwise perfectly translucid, when the latter are presented to them according to a determinate direction. The phenomenon thus presented is *polarization by refraction.*

Double refraction and polarization are qualities of crystals which are most intimately connected; and the combinations of these two manifestations produce magnificent phenomena of colouring, unattainable by substances producing simple refraction. It is very easy, by aid of a polariscope, to be assured upon the instant whether a precious stone possesses or not the power of double refraction.

Dichroism, polychroism, asteria.—The phenomena designated by these expressions, and which give a magical beauty to certain precious stones, are entirely due to the refraction and polarization of light. They show that the substances in which they are produced have not identically the same constitution in all their parts.

ELECTRICAL PROPERTIES.

In a general manner, all bodies acquire electricity by friction; only, one kind keep for a longer or shorter time the electricity confined as it were in their pores, while the other kind lose it instantly. The first are isolating bodies, the others are conducting bodies.

Precious stones belong to the first of these categories; but they exhibit great difference in the time during which they remain electrified; and this characteristic affords, in experienced hands, a very useful test for distinguishing one from another.

There are certain precious stones which possess the curious quality of becoming electric when they are subjected to heat. The tourmaline is especially susceptible to this thermotic electricity.

When precious stones are rubbed with the same material, usually a bit of cloth, some of them acquire positive electricity and the others negative electricity. Tourmaline, and other substances electrified by heat, usually exhibit positive electricity at one extremity and negative at the other.

OUTWARD CHARACTERISTICS.

TRANSPARENCY.

Transparency is the property that precious stones possess of being more or less easily traversed by luminous rays.

They are *transparent* when, being interposed between the eye and an object, they allow all the outlines of this object to be seen with perfect clearness. Example: the diamond.

They are *semi-transparent* when the objects viewed through them are a little confused. Example: the emerald.

They are *translucid* when nothing can be perceived when they are placed before the eye, but that the light evidently has a passage through them. Example: the chalcedony.

Finally, they are *opaque* when not a ray of light can penetrate them. Example: the jasper.

LUSTRE.

"Among minerals great differences are met with as regards the manner in which the light acts upon their surface. In this respect there are two separate effects to be distinguished, *lustre* and *colour*, which are one to the other as timbre is to sound in a musical instrument. Colour depends upon the nature of the reflected rays, lustre upon their intensity, and upon certain particular modifications of their tint which cannot be defined; it depends upon the structure of the body, its kind of texture, and the greater or less polish of its surface. Lustre, like colour and transparency, is susceptible of gradation; it is more or less vivid, more or less dull; and disappears entirely in varieties in which the aspect is rough, stony, or earthy" (Delafosse).

Adamantine lustre.—Intermediate between metallic lustre and vitreous lustre; it belongs to certain crystals; to the zircon, and above all to the diamond.

Nacreous or pearly lustre.—A mixture of silvery and vitreous lustre, resembling, as its name indicates, the nacre of pearl. Certain varieties of corundum possess this lustre in a very pronounced manner.

Silky lustre.—Due to straight fibres disposed very closely and of equal thickness. It resembles the sheen of certain fabrics of mohair.

Oily lustre.—The stones which possess this lustre are generally vitreous stones, which always seem, even when newly fractured, to have been impregnated with oil.

Resinous lustre.—A medium between the oily and the vitreous lustre. The opal generally presents this aspect.

Vitreous lustre.—This lustre recalls exactly the fracture of glass. It belongs generally to bodies in which the refracting power is inconsiderable.

ACTION OF LIGHT AND HEAT UPON PRECIOUS STONES.

Light.—When the most valuable precious stones, and the diamond particularly, are exposed for a certain time to the rays of the sun, and are then taken into darkness, they remain luminous, and exhibit the phenomenon of phosphorescence. This curious effect lasts for some time, but gradually becomes fainter and fainter, and finally disappears.

Heat.—The effects produced upon precious stones by heat are even more remarkable than those due to the action of light. Heat acts upon them in two very dissimilar ways. It modifies the elementary constitution of the stone by separating its molecules, but this in a manner altogether mechanical; or it produces in the stone a veritable chemical reaction. In the first case the modifications are temporary, and at length the objects return to their primitive condition; in the second case the effects produced are permanent.

As an example of the latter case, we may cite a practice whose origin is lost in antiquity, and which is still resorted to daily by lapidaries. It consists in submitting a coloured stone (diamond, topaz, &c.) to a temperature more or less elevated. Nearly always in these conditions the stone changes colour permanently.

A remarkable communication made to the Academy of Sciences will serve as an example of the first case.

"MM. Halphen have the honour to present to the Academy a diamond of the weight of 4 grammes (about 20 carats), presenting a phenomenon which has never been before observed, at least to their knowledge.

"This stone is, in its normal state, of a white colour, faintly tinged with brown. When it is subjected to the action of fire, it acquires a very clear rose-tint, which it retains for eight or ten days, and which it loses gradually, to return to its primitive normal colour.

"This change and return to the primitive state may be repeated indefinitely, for the diamond submitted to the Academy has been subjected five times to this test.

"The phenomenon in question arrested at first the attention of an observer, who was trying at random upon this diamond the prolonged action of fire. Experiments made since upon other diamonds have not produced the same result.

"This question of colouring diamonds has an importance which the Academy will easily appreciate, when it considers that the stone presented at this moment has, in its normal state, a value of 60,000 francs, while its price in the rose-coloured state, if the colour were permanent, would be from 150,000 to 200,000 francs."

PART II.

Historical Survey of Precious Stones. Ideas entertained by the Ancients, and in the mediæval age, concerning the Nature and Properties of Precious Stones. Their Classification based upon the analysis of Modern Chemistry.

"Though the same sun with all-diffusive rays
Blush in the rose, and in the diamond blaze,
We prize the effort of His stronger power,
And justly set the gem above the flower."

Brilliant objects have from time immemorial proved wonderfully fascinating to men. No wonder then that precious stones, those sparkling "blossoms of the rock," to whose rare beauty nature has added the crowning gift of durability, should have kindled a passion for possession and inspired ardent search.

In our own day the exceptional value of gems depends simply upon their use as ornaments, and their service in certain important optical and other instruments. With the ancients their importance rested on very different grounds. They attributed to these peerless little objects the most extraordinary gifts; they ascribed to them a spiritual as well as material potency—a power alike to cure diseases, to avert calamity, and to drive away the demons of the air.

The belief indeed came to prevail, that the presiding genius of a man's fate might be carried about with him in the shape of a precious stone. This superstition, though to us it appears so absurd, was

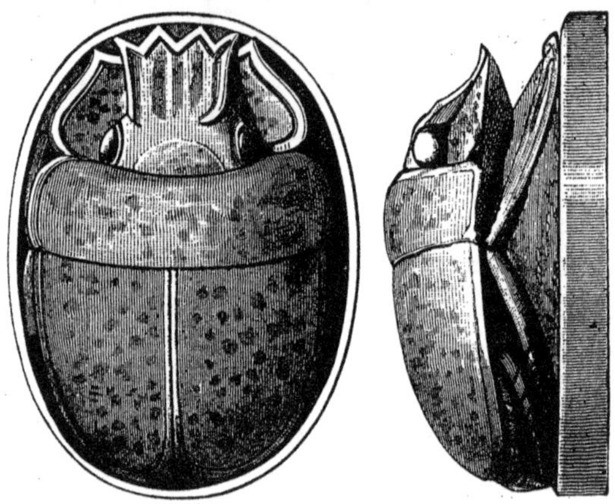

Fig. 19 —Egyptian Scarabæus cut in hard stone.

quite in accordance with the general views which then prevailed regarding the moral and physical worlds.

"A fact that governs all ancient history," says Hoefer, in his *Histoire de la Chimie*, "is the close alliance of religion with science. This alliance is one of the distinguishing characteristics of antiquity:

in it is found the solution of many of the problems that have disturbed the human mind."

It is this dominating fact that offers a key to the special history of precious stones.

Among the grand false or mistaken ideas held by the ancients, there are two that deserve all the attention of the historian and the philosopher. The first led them to consider man as a microcosm—a reduction in miniature of the entire universe, a 'little world' in exact counterpart of the 'great world.' Accordingly every part of man's body was believed to have a corresponding part in the vast universe.

The second was the conception of the soul of the world, according to which the souls of animated beings were but parts of the universal soul. At the moment of the dissolution of the body, said the philosophers of India, the soul, *âtmâ*, very different from the merely vital principle, will unite itself, if it is pure, with the great universal soul, *paramâtmâ*, from which it emanated. If it is impure it will be condemned to submit to a certain number of transmigrations, that is to say, to animate successively plants or animals, or *even to be incarcerated in some mineral body until,* purified of all imperfections, it is considered worthy of absorption, *mukti*, into the Divinity.

Thus minerals as well as animals and plants were to these philosophers *living beings.*

They maintained also, that the world was an animal reuniting the two principles, active and passive; an idea that entered fundamentally into nearly all the systems of ancient philosophy.

From India these theories passed into Egypt, whence they were transported to Greece by Plato, Pythagoras, and other philosophers. Confined for centuries to the European orient, they reappeared

Figs. 20 and 21.—Egyptian Figures carved in hard stone.

with some brilliancy at the commencement of the present era in the writings of philosophers of the school of Alexandria. In the mediæval age, when the alchemists transported them into the mineral kingdom, they reigned supreme.

If we examine, in connection with these ideas, the rank that was ascribed to precious stones, we shall find that they necessarily acquired a great importance. The beauty of their forms and the splendour of their colours could not fail to make them to be considered productions of an incomparable purity, and an epitome of all that nature held most perfect. To endow these marvellous products with properties in conformity with the prevailing idea of their nature and origin was but a step farther, and accordingly we find attributed to them talismanic virtues and agencies of the utmost potency.

Fig. 22.—Cornelian engraved: Egyptian.

"It would not be without interest," writes Babinet, "to follow the history of gems through that of humanity, from the ephod of Aaron to the pastoral cross of the Archbishop of Paris; from the offerings of rubies, sapphires, emeralds, diamonds, topazes, sardonyx, amethysts, carbuncles, and loadstones in

Fig. 23.—Egyptian Ring of Cornelian.

the temples of Jupiter and other pagan divinities, to the riches of the same nature which by the

sixteenth century had accumulated in what was called the 'treasury' of Christian churches. There is still preserved at Rome an emerald of Peru, sent in homage to the pope after the conquest of that country. It should be remarked, however, that these precious stores, originating in the piety of the

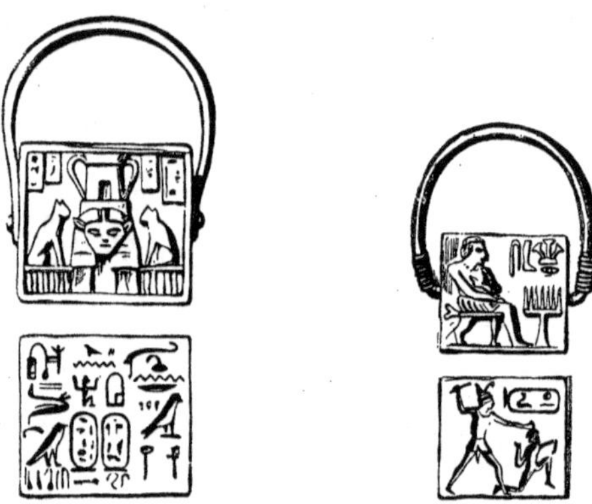

Figs. 24 and 25.—Egyptian Rings and Tablets engraved on both sides.

faithful, have not always been faithfully respected. When the reformation of Luther and Calvin in German countries, and later, the French revolution in countries remaining Catholic, transferred these votive riches to the possession of the civil authorities, it is well known that many fraudulent substitutions had been made, and that paste had frequently replaced the primitive gem."

"Precious stones," continues Babinet, "have in all times been highly esteemed, and without doubt will continue to be so in all ages to come. Comparing our modern luxury with the splendours of oriental courts and of Roman citizens enriched with the spoils of the world, we find ourselves inferior in many points, but not so far as diamonds are concerned. If in one of the brilliant réunions of the Tuileries, we calculate the value of the diamonds, even allowing deduction for false jewelry, we conclude that our French riches, although more widely spread, do not fall a whit behind the much-vaunted riches of Rome." And this remark applies with equal justice to the brilliant assemblies of other modern capitals.

The mythology of India refers to precious stones in terms that prove their general estimation in the most ancient ages: the songs and ballads of that country frequently mention these beautiful productions.

In Egypt a number of gems finely cut and engraved with consummate skill have been found beside mummies in tombs attributable to an extremely remote era. Their workmanship leads to the belief that the means employed by the ancient Egyptians in engraving hard stones did not differ sensibly from those used at the present day.

Types of these ancient jewels, copied from specimens in the museum of the Louvre, are represented by Figs. 19 to 25. Fig. 22 is particularly interesting; it is a red cornelian bearing hieroglyphic characters, exquisitely engraved.

The conquerors of Mexico found in the hands of the Incas a multitude of gems, cut and engraved with various images, which, according to Mexican traditions, had descended from a very remote period.

In the Bible there are several passages that refer with technical distinctions to precious stones. The most remarkable occurs in the description of the vesture of the high-priest, which was made, as the Scripture reads, "for glory and for beauty," and was adorned with symbolic gems. The ephod of Aaron was ornamented with two onyx stones, engraved with the names of the twelve tribes of Israel. The breast-plate consisted of twelve precious stones, set in the form of a double square, and of a size that allowed each stone, with its setting, to occupy a space of 2¾ ins. by 2 ins.

Translators differ in their rendering of the Hebrew names applied to these sacred stones—a fact which need not surprise us when we consider how few particulars are given—but the following order, although differing somewhat from the arrangement of Calmet, is in accordance with the opinion of the most celebrated rabbis.

Order of the Stones in Aaron's Breast-plate.

Primus Ordo.	1 *Oden.* Cornelian. REUBEN.	2 *Phideth.* Topaz. SIMEON.	3 *Barcketh.* Emerald. LEVI.
Secundus Ordo.	4 *Nophecth.* Ruby. JUDAH.	5 *Saphir.* Sapphire. ISSACHAR.	6 *Jaolam.* Diamond. ZEBULUN.
Tertius Ordo.	7 *Leschem.* Hyacinth. DAN.	8 *Schebo.* Agate. NAPHTALI.	9 *Achlamah.* Amethyst. GAD.
Quartus Ordo.	10 *Tarschisch.* Chrysolite. ASHER.	11 *Schoham.* Sardonyx. JOSEPH.	12 *Jaspeh.* Jasper. BENJAMIN.

In the book of Job there are facts mentioned that have led some to attribute to the author a profound knowledge of metallurgy; and he mentions by name the precious stones, sapphire, onyx, ruby, and topaz; crystal also, and coral and pearls. Mention is also made of geological phenomena similar to those which have played a part in bringing these mineral treasures to light, and which are so familiar to the geologists of the present day.

"He putteth forth his hand upon the rock; he overturneth the mountains by the roots; he cutteth out rivers among the rocks, and his eye seeth every precious thing. He bindeth the floods from overflowing, and the thing that is hid bringeth he forth to light."

In the New Testament the most remarkable passage in which precious stones are mentioned is that in the Apocalypse describing the New Jerusalem. "And the building of the wall of it was of jasper," we are told, "and the foundations of the wall of the city were garnished with all manner of precious stones." The precious stones were twelve in number, and they were arranged in order as below, where each has its colour placed opposite to it.

Order of Precious Stones in the Wall of the New Jerusalem (*Vision of St. John*).

Jasper	Dark opaque green.
Sapphire (*lapis lazuli*) .	Opaque blue.
Chalcedony	Greenish blue.
Emerald	Bright transparent green.
Sardonyx	White and red.
Sardius	Bright red.
Chrysolite	Bright yellow.
Beryl	Bluish green.
Topaz (or *Peridot*) . . .	Yellowish green.
Chrysoprasus	Darker shade of same.
Hyacinthus (*Sapphire*) .	Dark shade of azure.
Amethyst	Violet.

In the *Iliad* and *Odyssey* there are occasional metallurgic descriptions of much interest; and especially to be noted in regard to precious stones are the passages descriptive of the jewels of Juno.

MEDICAL MINERALOGY.

From the time of his first appearance upon the earth, man has been subject to malady and death. That is to say, medicine is as old as humanity.

It is probable that the earliest medicines were derived from vegetables, and that certain animal substances were next made use of; but it was long before people thought of employing mineral substances in medicine. This we first hear of in early Greek history.

Certain earths, generally aluminous, administered in various ways, were said to produce salutary effects. These earths were sold in little packages marked with different names, generally referring to the places of their origin. They were rendered still more efficacious by having a special seal affixed to them by the priests of various divinities, whence the term *terra sigillata* (*sigillum*, a seal). Among the most celebrated of these "sealed earths" was the earth of Lemnos, sold by the priestesses of the temple of Ephesus, in packages stamped with a goat, the sacred seal of Diana.

In the ancient pharmacopœias, precious stones are counted among the most valuable remedies. Special virtues were attributed to the ruby, topaz, emerald, sapphire, and hyacinth, which were rendered famous in medicinal annals under the title of "The Five Precious Fragments."

ASTROLOGICAL MINERALOGY.

Astrological mineralogy had its origin in Chaldea. A work of Abolays, translated by Jehuda Mosca about the middle of the thirteenth century, contains a catalogue of 325 stones, distributed by the Chaldean astronomers among the twelve signs of the zodiac, according to the relationship supposed to exist between the different stones and the constellations.

Later a single stone was specially consecrated to each sign of the zodiac, and consequently to each month of the year.

An amulet was made of these twelve sacred stones; so that as the constellations appeared successively above the horizon, the corresponding gems might always be on hand, to convey to the possessor the benign influences which they were then supposed to bestow.

The following list comprises the twelve stones of the amulet, with their zodiacal signs and the months of the year to which they corresponded:—

Garnet	*Aquarius*	January.
Amethyst	*Pisces*	February.
Jasper	*Aries*	March.
Sapphire	*Taurus*	April.
Agate	*Gemini*	May.
Emerald	*Cancer*	June.
Onyx	*Leo*	July.
Cornelian	*Virgo*	August.
Chrysolite	*Libra*	September.
Aquamarine	*Scorpio*	October.
Topaz	*Sagittarius*	November.
Ruby	*Capricornus*	December.

It is exceedingly probable that the origin of this superstition is to be traced to the twelve precious stones contained in the breast-plate of the Jewish high-priest.

Traces of sacred, poetic, astrological, and medical mineralogy frequently appear collectively, or in turn, in the treatises—even the most scientific—that, from the time of Homer until now, have been written upon precious stones.

Herodotus, born 484 years before Christ, five centuries after Homer, has left us a great number of statements, and some of them very valuable, concerning mineral substances known in his time: but he does not make mention of any new substance appertaining to the class of precious stones.

In the poems of Orpheus, attributed also to Onomacritus, and, in any case, as old as 450 B.C., there is evidence that the Greeks already attributed supernatural qualities to precious stones.

In the following century Plato, whose vast intelligence embraced so many transcendental ideas, was led to examine the origin of precious stones. He believed that they were veritable living beings, produced by a sort of fermentation determined by the action of a vivifying spirit descending from the stars. He described the diamond, which he distinguished from other precious stones as being a kind of *kernel* formed in gold; and supposed that it was the noblest and purest part of the metal that had condensed into a transparent mass.

Aristotle, born just a century after Herodotus, touches upon minerals only incidentally, at the end of his four books on *Meteors*, and sheds upon them no new light.

Theophrastus, a pupil of Aristotle, wrote a treatise upon precious stones, only a part of which has reached us. Notwithstanding the defects of this work, in part attributable to the times and in part to the author, we are none the less indebted to Theophrastus for the description of a number of important mineral substances unknown before his time.

We find also in this writer an idea which, taken by itself, is very singular: he divides the stones into two categories—male and female. When the reader remembers what has been said above, however, he will understand that there is nothing in this idea that is not in harmony with the general ideas of the ancients.

Dioscorides, whose valuable writings appeared in the first century of our era, furnishes, in a mineralogic point of view, no information of importance. But in another aspect his works are exceedingly interesting, seeing that we find in them the full development of the idea that precious stones possess a multitude of secret virtues—an idea admitted without dispute by all his successors, to a time very closely approaching our own, and which we find still entertained by the inhabitants of the mountainous regions of Spain and Arabia.

A few years after Dioscorides a work appeared, beyond all comparison in advance of its predecessors, the *Natural History* of Pliny. In this work, one of the most precious that we have inherited from antiquity, we find a chapter exclusively devoted to precious stones: it is a chapter to which we shall find occasion to refer in the following pages.

Leaving Pliny we must come down to the Arabs, ten centuries afterwards, before we find any new information upon minerals and precious stones. This we meet with first in the writings of Gerbert and Avicenna.

Avicenna acquired in his lifetime a wide reputation; and although it was due as much to his tact as to his science, it remained unrivalled for many centuries.

Among his writings there is a treatise upon stones, which comprehends results of great importance. The chapter devoted to the origin of mountains deserves particular notice. It is in this chapter that the learned Arab, always maintaining the hypothetical method of argument, expounds with an extraordinary grandeur and clearness of insight the theory of upheavals, that of Neptunism and of Plutonism, and the mode of formation of alluvial deposits: thus anticipating by eight centuries the results of modern science.

Two hundred years after Avicenna there appeared one of the grandest figures of the middle ages—Albertus Magnus, or Albert the Great.

Among the great works that we owe to this gifted man, or at least to his impulse and direction, is a treatise upon minerals, of which the illustrious chemist M. Dumas has said, "That which characterizes the treatise *De Rebus Metallicis* is the learned, precise, and often elegant exposition of the opinions of the ancients and of the Arabs; it is the methodical discussion of these which discloses at once the practised writer and the attentive observer."

In this treatise Albertus Magnus discusses precious stones; and while devoting a considerable space to the extraordinary properties of these beautiful productions, he carefully distinguishes a certain number of them, and indicates methods of obtaining several sorts of false gems.

Another illustrious genius of the middle ages—the friend and disciple of Albertus Magnus—St. Thomas Aquinas, whose voluminous works even surpass in extent those of his master, has written a treatise upon the *Nature of Minerals*, in which some very curious passages occur, especially on the fabrication of artificial stones.

In glancing over the works of Arnault de Villeneuve, of Raymond Lully, of Paul of Canotanto, of Isaac the Hollander, &c., we find a certain amount of space devoted to precious stones; but no new idea worthy of note. Thus the end of the fifteenth century is reached, and we emerge from the medieval age.

Upon the threshold of the Renaissance a singular character appears, Jerome Cardan (born in 1501), who furnishes us with some valuable suggestions. Several works of Cardan, published after his death, contain some rather absurd passages; but in his treatise *De Subtilitate,* the careful student finds many ideas which prove that the author possessed great intelligence, and beneath an air of *bonhommie* a veritable sagacity.

Cardan designates under the generic name of *gems* all the brilliant stones, and reserves the name of *precious stones* for those which are not only brilliant, but rare, and of small dimensions. These precious stones he divides into three classes: 1st, those which are brilliant and transparent, as the diamond; 2d, those which are opaque, like the onyx; 3d, those which are formed by the conjunction of the two other kinds, as the jasper.

This is very nearly the same classification as that employed by Caire, three centuries after Cardan.

According to Cardan, precious stones are engendered ("in the same manner as the infant from the maternal blood") by juices that distil from precious minerals in the cavities of the rocks: the diamond, the emerald, and the opal from gold; the sapphire from silver; and the carbuncle, the amethyst, and the garnet from iron.

In enumerating the flaws or imperfections which may be presented by precious stones, he makes a remarkable reflection, and one which has been considered an ingenious plea for excusing certain well-known imperfections of his own.

"In precious stones," he says, "imperfections are in reality less common than in animals and vegetables; but they are more conspicuous in jewels, simply because their nature is more brilliant and more rare. For the same reason, great men appear to have more vices than common mortals; but this is a delusion and an error. The lustre of their fame and the splendour of their names render their faults only the more apparent; while the ignorant vulgar, under favour of their obscurity, escape having their vices noticed."

It was admitted without question, in the time of Cardan, that precious stones were living beings.

"And not only do precious stones live, but they suffer illness, old age, and death."

He then speaks of the different virtues possessed

by precious stones. The hyacinth preserves from thunder-storms and from pestilence, and induces sleep. This last quality was attributed to it by Albertus Magnus. Without precisely rejecting this notion, Cardan confesses that he carries ordinarily a very large hyacinth, and that it has never appeared to contribute anything towards making him sleep; but he adds immediately, and with perfect naïveté, that his hyacinth has not the true colour, and may possibly be far from good. It was also believed that the hyacinth increased riches, augmented power, fortified the heart, brought joy to the soul, &c.

He describes the turquoise, which, mounted in a ring, secures the horseman from all injury if he falls from his horse; and adds, "I have a beautiful turquoise which was given me for a keepsake, but it has never occurred to me to test its virtues, as I do not care, for sake of the experiment, to fall from my horse."

It is not necessary to multiply examples to give an idea of the remarkable properties ascribed to gems in antiquity, and in the middle ages. In discussing this subject M. Babinet makes the following striking remarks:—

"For all maladies of a nervous or moral nature, where imagination might exert a great influence, precious stones were certainly a sovereign remedy.

In saying to such an invalid that an emerald placed under his pillow would drive away melancholy, dispel nightmare, calm the palpitations of the heart, induce agreeable thoughts, bring success to enterprises, and dissipate the anxieties of the soul, a cure was certain to be effected simply by the faith which the invalid had in the efficacy of the remedy. The hope of cure in such affections is the cure itself; and in all the numerous cases where the mind has had an influence upon the bodily system, the imaginary cause must produce a very real effect. Finally, that eternal deception of the human spirit, which registers all the cures, but does not take into account the cases where the curative means have failed of their end, contributed to maintain the belief in the occult virtues of precious stones. It is not half a century ago since sufferers would borrow from rich families gems mounted in rings, to apply to afflicted parts. When the trinket was introduced into the mouth as a cure for toothache, sore throat, or ear-ache, the precaution was taken to secure it with a strong thread, lest it should be swallowed by the patient.

"It is unnecessary to say that if we are asked to-day, whither are gone all these beliefs which to our fathers were incontestable, we answer that they are gone with the 'lunar influences' so powerful in the time of Louis XIV., to take their place in the vast limbo of human errors."

It remains to us now to say a few words concerning the order that we shall follow in the particular description of precious stones.

In spite of all the discussions that have arisen on this subject, and the great number of classifications presented by different authors who have occupied themselves with the question, there does not exist, and there cannot exist, any general and natural classification of precious stones. The reason is very simple: these substances being what we may call *particular cases* in nature, it is not possible to arrange them *in series*. By choosing any one of their general characteristics, crystalline form, refraction single or double, composition, or commercial value, &c., the geometrician, the physicist, the chemist, and the merchant can easily establish a classification answering more or less completely to their special end; but this is not a natural classification.

Without discussing or criticizing the different methods proposed, we shall adopt in this book a classification based upon *chemical composition*.

If there should be placed upon a table a specimen of every kind of precious stone known at the present day, it would be possible to separate them immediately, according to their chemical composition, into three perfectly defined groups.

The first comprises a single precious stone, the diamond. Its constituent principle is *carbon*.

The second includes the sapphire, the ruby, the topaz, the amethyst, the emerald, &c.—stones of which *alumina* is the base.

The third comprises stones whose base is *silica*—the opals, the agates, &c.

Carbon, alumina, silica: this is the order of importance of the three substances which enter essentially into the composition of precious stones; and in this order we shall arrange the chapters devoted to the history of all the gems which each division includes.

But before studying these groups, two descriptive terms applied to precious stones should be explained, the terms *Oriental* and *Occidental.*

Originally these words were applied in their literal sense; but at the present time they are retained in commercial parlance, not to indicate the regions from which the precious stones are brought, but simply to establish between stones of the same name a comparative value. The most precious variety of any precious stone is called *Oriental,* and the inferior variety *Occidental,* whatever may be the countries in which they are found.

PART III.

> " Le Diamant! c est l'art de choses ideales,
> Et ces rayons d'argent, d'or, de pourpre et d'azur
> Ne cessent de lancer les deux lueurs égales
> De pensers les plus beaux, de l'amour le plus dure."

The diamond, which for a long time has been considered the most precious of gems, has been known from early antiquity.

Its name *adamant*, a name that can be recognized in nearly all its modern appellations, was given by the Greeks, and signifies "the indomitable."

The excessive hardness of the diamond quite justifies this designation; but we find from the authors of antiquity that the ancients attributed to this stone certain other properties that it can by no means lay claim to, such as that of not becoming warm when heat was applied to it, and above all, that of resisting, without breaking, the blow of a hammer. The latter property is mentioned both by Lucretius and Pliny, not to go farther back.

> . . . . " Adamantina saxa
> Primâ acie constant, ictus contemnere sueta."

"The test of all these diamonds," says Pliny, "is made upon an anvil by blows of the hammer, and their repulsion for iron is such that they make the hammer fly in pieces, and sometimes the anvil itself is broken." This error maintained its ground down to a very late period. Thus in the year 1476, when, after the battle of Morat, the Swiss soldiers seized upon the tent of Charles the Bold, they found in it, among other treasures, a certain number of diamonds, and in order to test whether they were genuine struck them with hammers and hatchets, and of course broke them in pieces.

The diamonds earliest known to the Romans were furnished by Ethiopia; but when Pliny wrote, during the first half century of our era, they had already been brought from India; and thenceforward, until the eighteenth century, no diamond mines were known but those of the East Indies—in the empire of the Mogul, and in the island of Borneo.

Then the discovery of the Brazilian diamond districts created an excitement throughout the world; and, considerably more than a century afterwards, the opening of the diamond-fields of South Africa, has once more "revolutionized the trade."

In 1829, in accordance with a judgment expressed by Humboldt, diamonds were found in the Ural Mountains; they have also been obtained from Sumatra, Java, South Carolina, Georgia, Alaska, Arizona, Mexico, and Australia; but the production has been of too isolated occurrence to indicate any new centres of commerce.

The accepted diamond countries of history and commerce are India, Brazil, and South Africa.

DIAMOND MINES OF INDIA.

First of all, for size and beauty, the Indian diamonds are famed: "diamonds of Golconda" have become a synonym for preciousness and brilliancy. These gems were brought, not from the immediate vicinity of the fortress of Golconda, but from the mines of Raolconda and other localities situated in the territory of the Golconda kings. The mines were many years ago ceded to the English, but they have long since been abandoned; and it is believed that they are exhausted. Their treasures, however, shine in the coronets of every nation of the globe.

Diamond localities are numerous in Hindostan, and in Borneo, whose "Landak" diamonds have been especially prized; but many of these localities have ceased to be productive, and their names are becoming obsolete. In Tavernier's time the Golconda mines employed 60,000 people, and had already proved so rich that, as Ferishta records, the Sultan Mahmoud (A.D. 1177–1206) left in his treasury more than four hundred pounds weight of these precious gems.

It is from the descriptions of Tavernier, a

French jeweller who travelled through Turkey, Persia, and the Indies in the latter part of the seventeenth century, that we derive the most vivid accounts of the Indian mines.

"I visited first," he writes, "a mine in the territory of the kings of Visapoor, in a place called *Raolconda,* five days from Golconda, and eight or nine from Visapoor.

"All around the place where the diamonds are found the ground is sandy and full of rocks, and covered with coppice, somewhat like the environs of Fontainebleau. In these rocks are numerous veins, sometimes half a finger, sometimes a whole finger wide; and the miners have little iron rods, crooked at the end, which they thrust into the veins to dislodge the sand or earth in which the diamonds are found. . . . After this part of the work is done, the earth and sand is passed through two or three washings, and is carefully searched to see if it have any diamonds. It is from this source that the clearest stones and those of finest water are taken. The only evil is, that to render more easy the extraction of the sand from the rocks, such strong blows are given with a great lever of iron, that they shock (*étonne*) the diamond and produce flaws."

Tavernier visited also the mine of Garree, seven days east from Golconda, and the diamond-yielding bed of the river Gooel, in the kingdom of Bengal.

He relates, with very picturesque and lifelike details, his various affairs with the diamond merchants; and announces the somewhat remarkable fact, that the chief negotiators in the sale of diamonds in India were boys not over sixteen years of age.

"It is pleasant," says Tavernier, "to see the children of these merchants, and of other people of the country, from the age of ten to that of fifteen or sixteen, coming every morning and seating themselves under a large tree in the market-place of the town. Each has his diamond weights in a little pouch hanging at one side, and at the other side a purse attached to his girdle, and containing, in some cases, as many as six hundred gold pagodas. There they sit and wait until some one comes to sell them diamonds, it may be from the vicinity, or from some other mine. When anyone comes with something for them he places it in the hands of the eldest of the boys, who is, as it were, the chief of the band. He looks at it, and hands it to the one next him, and so it passes from hand to hand till it return to the first, not a word being spoken by any of them; the eldest boy then asks the price, in order to make a bargain, if possible, and if he happen to buy it too dear he has to take it on his own account."

When evening comes the boys bring together all the stones they have bought, examine them, and arrange them according to their water, their weight, and their clearness. Then they put upon each its price, as near as possible that at which they would sell to the merchants, and by the latter price they see how much profit they will have. They now carry them to the large merchants, who have always great numbers of stones to assort, and all the profit is divided among the boys, the one who acts as their chief receiving one-fourth per cent. more than the others. Young as they are, adds Tavernier, they know the price of every stone so well that if any of them have made a purchase, and is willing to lose a half per cent., another will give him his money.

He describes the devices resorted to by jewel-dealers to conceal any defects there might be in their merchandise; and the skilful manner of planning the cutting so as to dispose of flaws.

From the very moment of its recognition, it would seem that the diamond quickened the wits of its possessor, and aroused an ambition of brilliant gain. Even the poor slave in the mines managed occasionally to elude the sleepless vigilance of the overseers, and conceal a valuable gem. Tavernier saw in one of the Indian mines a poor wretch who, to appropriate to himself a fine diamond of the dimensions shown in Fig. 27, had forced it into the corner of his eye in such a way as to conceal it completely.

Fig. 26.—View in a Diamond District of Brazil.

According to Heynes' account of the mines of Hindostan, the diamond is found in alluvial soil, or the most recent rocks. "Shallow pits are excavated to the diamond beds, which lie about eight

Fig. 27.—Size of a Diamond hidden by a slave in the corner of his eye.

feet below the surface of the soil, in a conglomerate of rounded stones under two distinct layers; the uppermost, a mixture of sand, gravel, and loam; and the other, thick black clay or mud."

DIAMOND MINES OF BRAZIL.

Brazilian diamonds are found in the district of Minas Geraes, at San Paulo, in the beds of various rivers, and at Serro Frio, or Cold Mountain, a lofty plateau measuring eight leagues by sixteen. The most productive districts of late are Matto Grosso and Bahia.

The diamonds occur usually in alluvial soil, enveloped in a conglomerate formed of rounded white quartz pebbles and light-coloured sand. The miners have names for each variety of soil; as—

Grupiara, the unused bed of a river.

Burgalhoa, angular fragments of rocks that strew the ground; and

Cascalho, the generic name of all.

When diamonds were first found by the gold hunters of Brazil, no notion was formed of their value. They were used for counters in card-playing. But at last a native named Bernardo Lobo, who had journeyed to the East Indies, and had seen uncut diamonds there, recognized the nature of these disregarded pebbles.

The news of the discovery spread across the world, and its first effect was a panic in the diamond trade. Some time had to elapse before the dealers in Indian gems could reconcile themselves to any rival that might depreciate the treasures of the Orient.

Meanwhile upon the inhabitants of the diamond districts the discovery acted like a curse; and to the bitter sorrows of persecution were added the horrors of earthquake and drought. "It seemed as if the genii," says Emmanuel, "guardians of the treasure, were indignant at the presumption of man, and tried by every means to prevent the dispersion of the buried treasure."

But the riches of the province were incalculable. The search for gold no longer offered any attraction; the children gathered the precious dust after the rains. The energies of the gold-hunters were

Fig. 28.—First wash of the Diamond-yielding Soil in Brazil.

diverted to diamond finding; care was taken even to examine the crops of all kinds of killed fowls, for diamonds had been found in this way; a negro found a gem of five carats adhering to a cabbage which he had plucked for his dinner.

As the search became organized, the waters of the rivers were diverted at the dry season into canals. The soil was dug to the depth of about ten feet, and deposited in heaps near the washing huts. These huts were furnished with elevated seats for the overseers, who watched incessantly the long troughs, called *canoes*, in which the *cascalho* was washed.

When a slave found a diamond of 18 carats he received his freedom, and was crowned with flowers, and led in a triumphal procession, amid the rejoicings of his friends.

Modern appliances and innovations have altered somewhat the primitive modes of diamond washing, but the leading features remain the same, the object being to wash away the finer particles of soil, and obtain the gems from the residue.

In 1754, a slave, transported from Minas Geraes to Bahia, discovered, from analogies of soil that led to immediate diamond-seeking, the wonderfully rich district of Bahia. It is now estimated that the Brazils export annually from Rio Janeiro an amount of rough diamonds averaging in value from four to five millions of dollars.

DIAMOND MINES OF SOUTH AFRICA.

In the autumn of 1868 news reached England from Capetown that diamonds had been found in the gold districts on Orange River, midway between the eastern and western coasts of South Africa. And in the spring of the following year all doubts that had been either genuine, or instigated by jealous fear of disturbance in the diamond trade, were silenced by the discovery of the "African Koh-i-noor," valued at about $150,000.

This splendid stone, destined to create a stir that should widen into the most distant circles, was found by a poor herdsman, who had the supreme happiness to dispose of it for five hundred sheep, ten head of cattle, and a horse. It was taken to Capetown, where an injunction was placed upon it by emissaries of Waterboer, chief of the Griquas, who claimed it as the possession of his own territory; but, for lack of proof, the injunction was removed, and the diamond finally reached England. From that time tidings of new discoveries became more and more frequent; and the Griquas began successfully to search the beds of their streams.

By 1870 public attention had become thoroughly aroused. Already enterprising men and capitalists, among them Coster of Amsterdam, were on the field. The diamond districts of the Vaal had proved an entire success. Seventy-two large diamonds were found at Pniel in one week; ninety-one were unearthed by a single digger within a fortnight; diamonds to the amount of $500,000 had been picked up by Europeans.

A regular organization of diggers was formed near the mission station of Pniel,—itself, as afterwards proved, one of the richest localities. A "digging committee" apportioned to each man so many square feet, to be worked at once or abandoned. The diamond claims of these "dry diggings" came eventually to be sunk sixty feet below the surface; sometimes seventeen feet of red sand was removed before diamondiferous soil could be reached. The best yield occurred generally at the depth of twenty or twenty-five feet. The natives worked in these pits with pick and shovel; above them were the sorting-tables, some under cover, some not; and between the crowded pits carts crawled along, bringing burdens of gravel to the tables, to be sorted by the Europeans.

The excitement had now reached its height. Not only did every town of South Africa empty itself of men for "the diggings," but diamond-hunters made their appearance from every quarter of the globe. There were forty thousand people within a line of seventy miles upon the banks of the Vaal

River. Hotels, shops, music-halls flourished; two newspapers were started. One after another new diamond-fields were brought to light. Du Toit's Pan, De Beers, Pniel, New Rush, and Colesberg Kopje opened their dazzling mines.

The rival claims of different routes from the coast were contested with the utmost zeal. Railways and telegraphs were projected, and modern machines were hastened to the scene. The mines were pronounced the richest in the world. Diamonds weighing from 20 to 30 carats were not unusual; and among the exceptional treasures found were diamonds weighing considerably more than 100 carats; including the beautiful "Star of Beaufort," and the "Star of Diamonds," weighing 107½ carats; and a lovely stone, which attracted especial attention by exhibiting, under the microscope, an aspect of pointed mountain summits, lighted by vivid sunlight with all the colours of the rainbow. Rubies and turquoises were also found.

But all these successes were not unalloyed. There were droughts, and fevers, and mournful death-lists. There were threatened invasions of the Caffres that kept all the white men armed; and frauds that occasioned lynch-law mobs; and annoyances on the frontiers. And there were endless disputes of boundaries and territorial rights, not altogether quelled when, to the joy of the miners, the British flag was hoisted on the diamond-fields, Nov. 1871; and the district south and west of the Vaal, known as West Griqualand, was proclaimed under the protection of the crown.

The South African diamonds are found over many hundred square miles of territory. The principal diggings are situated in the extensive valley of the Vaal river, to the north-east of the Orange River Free State, and within the boundary of the Cape Colony as now defined. The country here rises into long stony ridges, called *kopjes*, consisting of irregular fragments of hard rock imbedded in ferruginous gravel, which varies in character and compactness, being sometimes quite loose and sometimes forming a compact lime-cemented mass. It is in this gravel that the diamonds are found. They occur at various depths down to twenty feet or more, but the usual depth is from two to six feet below the surface. "The manner of working is simple enough. A claim, or piece of ground thirty feet square, is occupied by two diggers in partnership, assisted by their black servants. They remove the loose blocks of stone, which are cast aside; they take up the gravel and sift it thoroughly, either in a dry state, or with abundance of water in a sieve rocked by a cradle. When the pebbles have been thus separated from the sand, they are cleansed, and placed upon the sorting-table to be carefully examined for any diamonds that may lie among them."

Some fears were entertained as 1872 opened with still brightening prospects, that the large numbers of stones found might produce a depreciation in value; but such is the unprecedented demand for diamonds, these fears have not yet been realized. The "off colour" of South African diamonds only enhances the value of the translucent and colourless stones of Brazil and India; and their large size and extreme brilliancy finds for them an ample appreciation. It is estimated that the diamonds exported from Capetown during the year 1871 amounted in value to $7,500,000.

WEIGHT AND VALUE OF DIAMONDS.

The diamond is known in three different molecular states, forming a graduated series that is very remarkable. It is *crystallized*, *crystalline*, and *amorphous*.

The crystallized diamond is the diamond "par excellence;" it is that which, when cut, is used in jewelry.

The crystalline diamond cannot be cut. It bears in commerce the name of "boart," and is reduced to powder for cutting crystallized gems.

The amorphous diamond is of a steel-gray colour

and quite opaque. It occurs in sandstone of very old formation, and is found in Bahia, and of late in Mexico. It has no utility when cut, but reduced to powder it is used for polishing diamonds and other gems, and is especially prized by the watchmakers of Switzerland. Its hardness is identical with that of the crystallized diamond; its specific gravity is 3·012 to 3·016. It is not used to so good advantage in proportion to its weight as "boart." It is known in commerce under the name of *carbonate*, or *carbonic diamond.*

Crystallized diamonds in their natural state are called "rough diamonds."

The diamond is always sold by weight. The standard of weight for all precious stones is the *carat;* a name derived, it is said, from the seeds of a pod-bearing plant used in the East to measure gold dust. The carat is 4 grains; that is, diamond grains, which differ slightly from troy grains, as it takes five of the former to weigh four of the latter; or more exactly, one carat = 3·174 gr. troy.

The carat is universally employed in the commerce of jewelry, but it is not rigorously the same in all countries. The following are the weights of the different carats in milligrammes:—

Brazil,	205·750
France,	205·500
England,	205·409
Holland,	205·044
Spain,	205·393

The carat is divided into $\frac{1}{2}$, $\frac{1}{4}$, $\frac{1}{8}$, $\frac{1}{16}$, $\frac{1}{32}$, $\frac{1}{64}$ of the carat. The table of weights of a jeweller's balance should contain from the weight of a thousand carats to these fractions.

The balance employed by dealers in precious stones is a simple little balance which is held in the hand: and yet "such is the experienced quickness of the lapidary," says M. Helphen, "that the balance of the assayer will never find him wrong by even the 64th part of a carat."

Rough crystallized diamonds are valued at from 16½ to 19 dollars the carat, for assorted lots containing no diamonds of more than one carat. Above this weight prices are a different affair.

The rule made known two hundred years ago by Tavernier, that "the prices of two diamonds are proportioned to the squares of their weights," is endorsed by some modern lapidaries. According to this rule, since a one-carat stone of the first water, well cut and without flaws, is valued at about $93, a stone of two carats should be worth four times that, or $372; and one of three carats, nine times as much, or $837.

But statistics show that this rule, which was quite true in the time of Jeffries and Tavernier, is no longer applicable; it assigns to diamonds a higher price than in commerce they really bring.

A table is given here, which not only establishes this fact, but which also furnishes other interesting conclusions. It is a table showing the prices of diamonds in the years 1606, 1750, 1865, and 1867.

COMPARATIVE VALUES OF DIAMONDS IN 1606, 1750, 1865, AND 1867.

BRILLIANTS.	1606.	1750.	1865.	1867.
	Dols. cts.	Dols. cts.	Dols. cts.	Dols. cts.
½ carat, ...	—	—	25 48	28 08
¾ ,, ...	—	—	44 26	51 52
1 ,, . . .	101 37	37 57	84 25	98 39
1¼ ,, ...	172 42	58 59	131 31	164 05
1½ ,, ...	273 97	84 44	178 18	210 92
1¾ ,, ...	354 88	114 57	225 06	257 79
2 ,, ...	405 85	150 10	304 85	375 16
2¼ ,, ...	456 81	189 53	328 29	422 03
2½ ,, ...	558 55	234 36	453 46	516 15
2¾ ,, ...	761 48	283 27	468 90	562 65
3 ,, ...	914 37	337 59	586 08	656 39
3¼ ,, ...	—	—	632 95	703 26
3½ ,, ...	1015 56	395 80	703 26	821 19
3¾ ,, ...	—	—	821 19	890 94
4 ,, ...	1219 04	459 42	—	—
4¼ ,, ...	—	—	1078 42	1125 30
4½ ,, ...	1421 97	677 04	1172 17	1406 71
4¾ ,, ...	—	—	1312 97	1547 33
5 ,, ...	1624 71	937 81	1500 46	1641 07

VALUES OF DIAMONDS IN 1872

(*A Table prepared by* Mr. HERMANN, *President of the New York Diamond Company*).

Melée, per carat, ... from $60 to $65
Melange, ,, ... ,, $100 to $110

VALUE OF BRILLIANTS IN CURRENCY.

Brilliants of		Brilliants of	
½ carat, ...	$35	3 carats, ...	$500 to $550
¾ ,, ...	60	3¼ ,, ...	600 to 650
1 ,, ...	100 to $125	3½ ,, ...	700 to 750
1¼ ,, ...	150 to 175	3¾ ,, ...	800 to 850
1½ ,, ...	200 to 225	4 ,, ...	900 to 950
1¾ ,, ...	250 to 275	4¼ ,, . . .	1000 to 1050
2 ,, ...	300 to 325	4½ ,, ...	1100 to 1150
2¼ ,, ...	350 to 375	4¾ ,, ...	1200 to 1250
2½ ,, ...	400 to 425	5 ,, ...	1300 to 1400
2¾ ,, ...	450 to 500		

The prices of the preceding table refer only to diamonds of the first quality, and without a flaw.

One sees immediately that the rule of Tavernier is completely at fault. For by his rule the value of the one carat, being estimated in 1867 at $98, 39c., a diamond of two carats should have been worth $393, 56c., while in reality it brought $375, 16c.; and a diamond of five carats should have been worth twenty-five times as much, $2459, 75c., when it brought actually only $1641, 7c.

Another point that strikes the attention in inspecting this table, is the extraordinary depression in the price of diamonds in the middle of the eighteenth century. It was about that time that the discovery of the diamond districts of Bahia occasioned a panic in the diamond market.

Lastly, the table shows that, *absolutely*, the price of diamonds was nearly the same in 1606 as in 1867; but when we take into account the difference in the value of money at these two epochs, we see that diamonds were really much dearer at the beginning of the seventeenth century than they are now.

Fig. 29.—Dimensions of a Brilliant of 10 carats.

Large diamonds are exceedingly rare. It is estimated that among ten thousand diamonds hardly one will be found of ten carats weight; that is to say, of the size represented by Fig. 29.

COMPOSITION OF THE DIAMOND.

The ancients had no suspicion of the true nature of the diamond. To have any idea of this subject, it was necessary that the bases of modern chemistry should be established, or at least that the complex phenomenon of combustion should have received its true explanation. Newton suspected from its wonderful refractive power that the diamond was combustible, but even as late as the middle of the eighteenth century, the definition of its composition, given in a standard work on physics, was—"the purest and finest *earth*, the most ethereal *fire*, and the most limpid *water*."

The first important fact relative to the nature of the diamond was established by Boyle about the middle of the seventeenth century. He showed that under the influence of a great heat the diamond disappeared. A little later, in 1694, Cosmo III., Grand-duke of Tuscany, had a diamond subjected at Florence to the intense heat of the sun's rays, by aid of a concave mirror. The experiment was conducted by Averini, preceptor of the Prince John Gaston, son of Cosmo, and Targioni, member of the Academy *del Cimento*. The diamond first split, then emitted sparks, and finally disappeared.

This experiment was repeated at Vienna by Francis Stephen of Lorraine, afterwards Francis I. of Austria. The sun's rays were replaced by the fire of a furnace, with the same result. Nearly a hundred years after the experiment at Florence it was renewed in Paris by D'Arcet, Rouelle, and Macquer. On the 26th of July, 1771, these savants burned in the laboratory of Macquer a beautiful diamond furnished by an amateur, Godfrey de Villetaneuse. That the diamond had disappeared was certain, but the question arose whether it had actually burned or was merely volatilized.

In the midst of the discussion, Le Blanc, a celebrated jeweller of the day, ignoring the experiments carried out at Florence, Vienna, and Paris, affirmed that fire had no effect upon the diamond. He had frequently, he said, submitted diamonds to a high temperature to remove certain defects, and the heat had never in the least degree deteriorated the stone.

To prove his assertion he tried an experiment before a great number of spectators in the laboratory of Rouelle. He enveloped a diamond in a mixture of lime and charcoal dust, introduced it into a crucible, and exposed it to a violent heat. After about three hours the interior of the crucible was examined, and nothing was found there but the little box that the diamond had occupied. The experiment had resulted like the others, and Le Blanc retired amid the acclamations of his opponents, "without his diamond, but still unconvinced."

Light had now begun to dawn upon the question, but it was still far from being settled. Accordingly Cadet, Macquer, and the illustrious Lavoisier made preparations for new experiments on the subject, when a skilful lapidary named Maillard presented himself before them, and maintained, as Le Blanc had done, that fire had no effect on the diamond. He offered to submit three diamonds to the most prolonged and intense heat, but he stipulated that he should be allowed to carry out the experiment in his own way.

This being granted, Maillard took the bowl of a tobacco-pipe, placed the three diamonds in it in the midst of charcoal powder closely packed, closed the mouth of the pipe with a cover of iron, and then shut up the whole in a crucible filled with chalk and covered with a siliceous coating. (See Fig. 30.) The crucible was now subjected to a temperature such that at the end of four hours it was completely soft and on the point of melting, when the fire was slackened. After the crucible had been allowed to cool it was carefully broken open, the pipe-bowl was found to be entire, with the charcoal in it as black as at first; and in the midst of this the three diamonds, in every respect unaltered and uninjured.

Some diamonds prepared by Maillard, and submitted for twenty-four hours to the enormous tem-

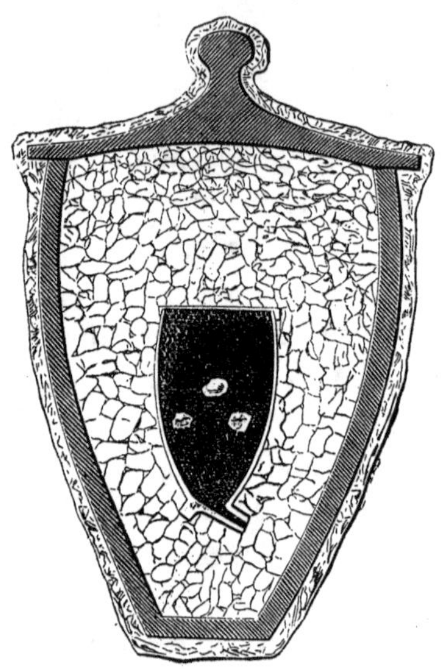

Fig. 30.—Maillard's Experiment.

perature of a porcelain furnace, resisted the heat like the preceding.

Analogous experiments were made in different parts of Europe, sometimes with the one, sometimes with the other of the preceding results. The facts remained inexplicable till—on the principal phenomena of combustion being established—it was noticed that the diamond had always disappeared when it had been heated in the presence of air, while it had undergone no modification when removed from the action of the air by means of substances such as powdered charcoal, lime, &c.

Arrived at this stage, the question could not long remain unsolved; and the solution was soon furnished by two of the creators of the science of chemistry—Humphry Davy in England, and Lavoisier in France.

"And what is the diamond?" asks Babinet, who has such a quick eye to the poetry of science. "The most precious thing in the whole world. And what is carbon? The most common material that is known; one that not only exists in vast quantities in the bowels of the earth, but that plants and trees of every kind contain, in an inconceivable quantity. Silver can hardly pay for the diamond; for if we imagine a diamond of the weight of a twenty-five franc piece, it would weigh about 125 carats, and cost at least four millions of francs; while an equal weight of carbon, even having recourse to the smallest copper pieces, would have no appreciable value. And yet the diamond and carbon are identical. Diamond is crystallized carbon."

Everyone knows the pungent gas that escapes from fermented liquors—cider, beer, wine, &c.—and

is introduced artificially into aerated waters. It is formed by the combination of carbon with one of the elements of the air (oxygen), and is called by chemists *carbonic acid.* This substance is produced whenever carbon, or substances which contain carbon, are burned in contact with the air; and not the slightest trace of it is ever found, if the substance burned does not contain carbon.

After this grand fact had been established, it was very easy to find out if the diamond contained carbon, and also whether this was its sole constituent. To settle the first question, the celebrated Lavoisier had recourse to the experiment represented by Fig. 31.

A bell-glass filled with oxygen was reversed in a basin containing mercury. A cupel placed at the extremity of a little column received the diamond, upon which the sun's rays were concentrated by means of a burning-glass.

The diamond disappeared; and it was proved that the glass, which at the commencement of the experiment had contained no trace of carbonic acid, contained a great quantity after the disappearance of the diamond. The diamond then contained carbon as one of its elements. Davy did not remain satisfied with this.

By analogous experiments he showed that the combustion of the diamond in oxygen produced carbonic acid only; the diamond, then, must be composed of carbon and nothing else.

Certain doubts still lingered upon this point, but they were dispelled by the publication in 1841 of

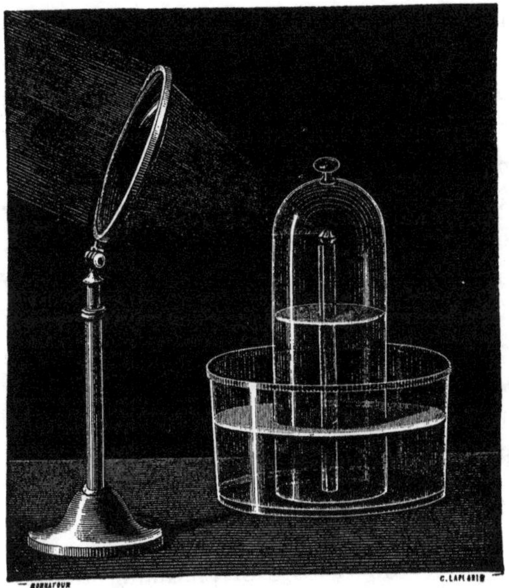

Fig. 31.—Combustion of the Diamond by Lavoisier.

the grand work of MM. Dumas and Stass upon the equivalent of carbon.

In their experiments these two savants burned a great number of diamonds, but they corrected an error the maintenance of which would have been a veritable calamity to science. The capital importance of the results obtained by MM. Dumas and Stass completely justified the use of such exceptional fuel.

It is very probable that the absolutely pure diamond consists exclusively of carbon; but perfectly pure diamonds are very rare. All those burned by MM. Dumas and Stass left a residuum or ash, if we may call it so, sometimes in the form of a spongy network of a reddish-yellow colour, sometimes as crystalline particles of a straw-yellow colour, sometimes as colourless and crystalline fragments. This residuum varied from $\frac{1}{500}$ to $\frac{1}{2000}$ of the weight of the diamond employed.

It used to be believed that the diamond could be consumed only with great difficulty. This error is corrected by one of the most fascinating experiments of chemistry. It was first performed by M. Morren, senior of the faculty of sciences at Marseilles.

Fig. 32.

He took a wire of platinum, and by means of a little cone of wood gave it the shape represented by Fig. 32.

He then fixed the upper end of the wire in a cork, and placed in the little receptacle the diamond to be burned. A phial filled with oxygen was at hand. By aid of a blowpipe the temperature of the diamond and its support was elevated to white heat, and then was plunged quickly into the phial of oxygen (Fig. 33). The diamond immediately kindled, and continued to burn with a steady glow infinitely more vivid than that which could have been obtained from any other variety of carbon.

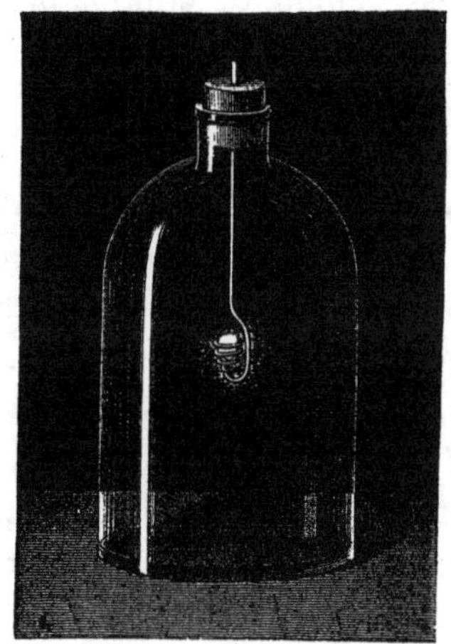

Fig. 33.—Combustion of the Diamond in Oxygen.

M. Morren has also proved that the diamond burns in layers: for if the combustion is arrested at any period, the special system of crystallization is still regularly displayed.

This is a very important point, since it excludes all idea of fusion for the diamond.

CELEBRATED DIAMONDS.

It is from Asia, that cradle of luxury and splendour, that most of the diamonds that have become famous have been derived.

Tavernier gives a minute description of the diamonds of Aurengzebe, at whose court he was favourably received, and whose jewels he was permitted to inspect and weigh.

"The first stone," he writes, "that Akel-Kau placed in my hands was a great diamond cut as a rose, very high on one side. It had a slight notch on one of its edges, and a small flaw within. It was of the first water, and weighed 280 carats." When brought from the mine of Colore, near Golconda, it weighed 787½ carats, but had several flaws. Hortensio Borghis, a Venetian, was employed to cut it, and the work nearly cost him his life; for the king accused him of having spoiled the diamond, and only allowed him the privilege of retaining his head on the payment of ten thousand rupees. This diamond is believed to be the same as that which now belongs to Queen Victoria, and is known as the Koh-i-noor. Its history will be given below.

"After having fully examined this beautiful stone," continues Tavernier, "and having returned it to the hands of Akel-Kau, he showed me another diamond, finely formed, and of the first water, with three table-cut diamonds, two clear, and one having little black points. Each one of these weighed from 48 to 50 carats; and the first 54½ carats. He then showed me a trinket consisting of twelve diamonds all roses, and each one weighing from 13 to

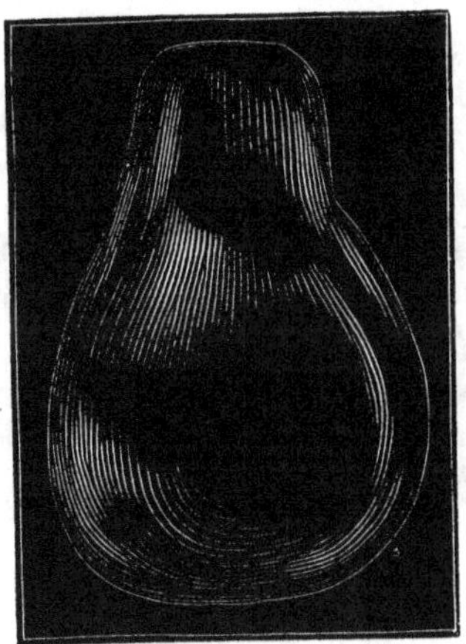

Fig. 34.—Diamond of the Rajah of Mattan.

14 carats. In the midst was a heart-shaped rose, of first water, with three little flaws: this rose weighed 35 carats."

One of the most celebrated diamonds is that of the Rajah of Mattan, in Borneo. It was found on that island, and weighs 318 carats.[1] It is shaped

[1] Other accounts make the weight of this diamond 367 carats.

like a pear, and of the dimensions shown in Fig. 34.

This diamond is considered by the people of Borneo as a kind of palladium to which the destinies of the empire are attached. They attribute to it the miraculous power of curing all diseases

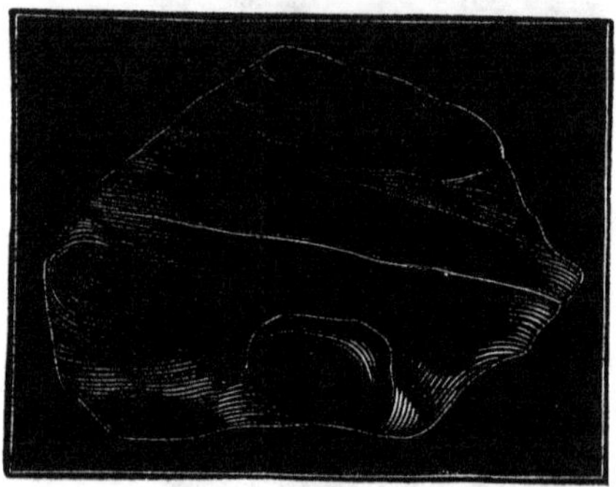

Fig. 35.—The Nizam.

by means of the water in which it has been dipped. On one occasion, according to Jamieson, the governor of Borneo offered for it $150,000, two large war-brigs with their guns and ammunition, a certain number of guns, and a quantity of powder and shot. But the rajah refused to part with it.

India has in its possession another famous diamond, the Nizam (Fig. 35), a rough diamond weighing 340 carats, and estimated at $930,000.

One of the most celebrated diamonds in the

world is the Regent or Pitt diamond. Its brilliancy and proportions are considered matchless, and it is also of considerable size. It was found in the mine of Parteal, forty-five leagues south of Golconda, and weighed in the rough state 410 carats. Two years and $23,250 were spent in cutting it into a brilliant

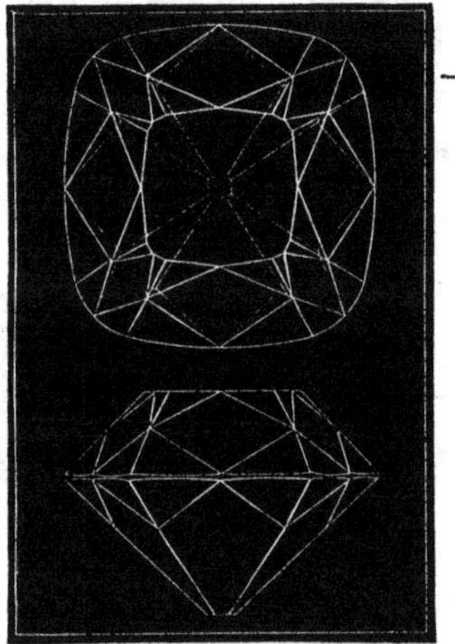

Fig. 36.—The Regent.

—a process which reduced it to 137 carats, but the cutting is perfect.

The usual account given of this diamond is, that it was bought at Madras by the grandfather of the first Earl of Chatham, when he was commander of Fort St. George; that he paid $60,000 for it, and that it was bought in 1717 for $648,000 by the

Duke of Orleans, when regent of France during the minority of Louis XV.

A very different story, however, is told by Saint-Simon, who professes to speak of his own personal knowledge.

He says that the diamond was stolen by a person employed in the diamond mines, who escaped to Europe with it, and after showing it to several princes, and among the rest the King of England, passed over to Paris and showed it to the somewhat notorious Law. Law proposed to the regent that it should be bought for the king, but the state of the finances was such that the duke hesitated to spend such a large sum in that way. Saint-Simon lent his influence in favour of the purchase, representing that the diamond was peerless in Europe, and would well become the crown of France, and that the purchase of it would shed glory on the regency of the duke. The latter at last consented, and the diamond was bought for $384,000, the seller receiving also the fragments resulting from the cutting, with interest on the price until the whole was paid.

From that time the Regent became identified with the fortunes of France, and a chapter of historic details belongs to its career. It has passed through many revolutions, and it has passed—very literally—through many hands; for in the days that followed the fall of Louis XVI., the Regent, carefully chained and guarded by gendarmes, was exposed to the people of Paris; and any half-starved workman who chose might hold this symbol of royal splendour and epitome of twelve million francs for a few moments in his brown hand.

The Regent—pawned to the Batavian government by Napoleon I.—stolen by robbers, and its hiding-place revealed at the gate of death by one

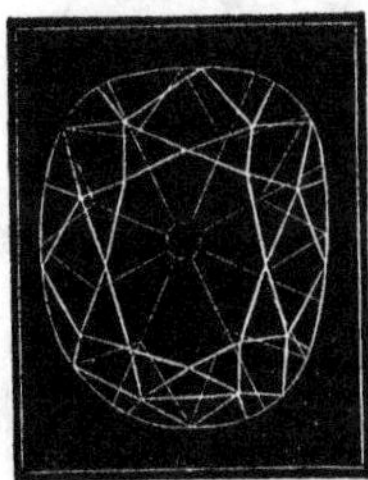

Fig. 37.—Empress Eugénie.

of the reckless band, and mounted in the state sword of the first Napoleon—finally glittered in the imperial diadem, through the palmy days of Napoleon III.

Another beautiful diamond is the Empress Eugénie. It is cut as a brilliant, and weighs 51 carats.

A third famous diamond, belonging for some time to France, is the Sancy. Its history is not quite certain. According to some authorities it was brought by an ambassador from Constantinople; according to others, it ornamented the helmet of Charles the Bold, who lost it at the battle of Granson. It was found by a Swiss soldier, who sold it to a priest for two francs; it disappeared then for some time, until, in the year 1589, King Anthony of Portugal pledged it among other stones to De Sancy, then treasurer of the King of France, who retained it by paying 100,000 livres

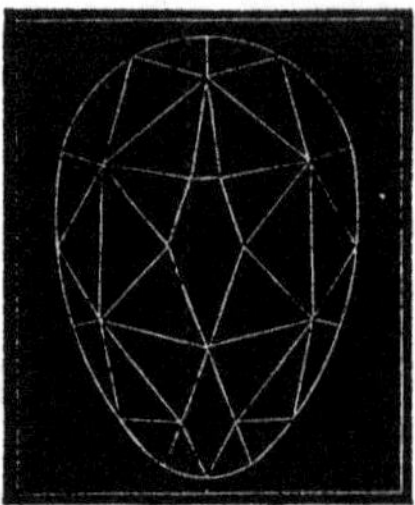

Fig. 38.—The Sancy.

(coinage of Tours). Henry III., after a lapse of time, borrowed it for the purpose of pledging it to the Swiss government; but the servant who was carrying it to the king disappeared, and was not heard of for some time. At last it was discovered that he had been assassinated in the forest of Dôle, and buried by the care of a charitable curé in the cemetery of a village. "Then," said the Baron de Sancy, "my diamond is not lost." In fact the gem was found in the stomach of the servant, whose fidelity had given him at the last moment the presence of mind to swallow it.

According to the inventory of 1791 the Sancy weighed $33\frac{12}{16}$ carats. It excited especial interest from the peculiarity of its cutting.

In 1792 the Sancy once more disappeared, and was found by the police of Paris, through an anonymous letter, in the Champs Elysées. It is now in Russia, and is valued at what M. Helphen considers an exaggerated price, $186,000.

The crown-jewels of France, including the Regent and the Sancy, contained in 1774, 7482 diamonds. This magnificent collection was stolen in 1792.

The collection of Napoleon I., gathered from every part of Europe, was superior to the old collection, but inferior to the one subsequently made, which contained 64,812 diamonds, in 1832, valued at $3,887,848. After that time there was again an increase in the number of the French jewels, including the beautiful Empress Eugénie.

Within a year, according to statistics of 1872, the Bonaparte family alone have thrown upon the market diamonds to the amount of $1,210,000.

Brazil, rich in mines of precious stones, would naturally be supposed to possess valuable jewels; and in fact the crown diamonds of this empire are valued at more than $18,600,000.

Among the principal diamonds is that which, cut in a pyramid, adorns the handle of the cane of John VI., and is estimated at $162,192. Brazil has furnished also the twenty diamonds which form the twenty buttons of the doublet of ceremony of Joseph I., each one of which is valued at $23,250; the whole costume representing a sum of $465,000.

But the marvel among these productions of Brazil is the Star of the South. This extraordinary diamond was found in 1853 in the mines of Bogagan, by a poor negress. The rough diamond weighed 257½ carats. It has been purchased by M. Helphen.

This beautiful diamond has now been cut. It is of an irreproachable purity, transparent, and taking by refraction a lovely rose tint.

The Star of the South was cut at Amsterdam in the establishment of M. Coster; and no better example could be given of the difference between a rough diamond and one that has been cut, than is presented by Fig. 39, in which the different views of the Star of the South, in its rough state, are taken from drawings made by the illustrious mineralogist M. Dufrénoy. Figures are also given of the diamond as it now appears.

Among the diamonds found in Brazil are three famous stones belonging to the crown of Portugal.

The first is called the King of Portugal's diamond. It was found in a place called Cay-de-Mérin, near the little river of Malhoverde. Mawe

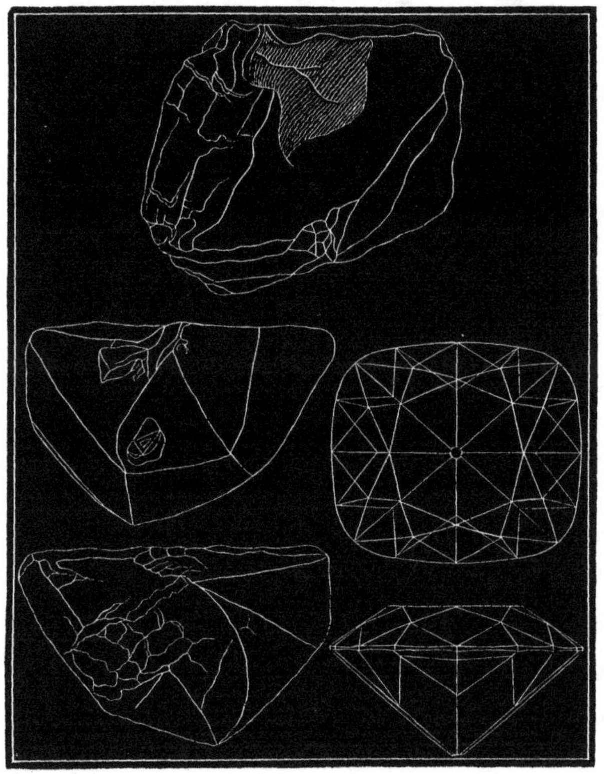

Fig. 39 — Star of the South, before and after cutting.

says that it weighs 1680 carats. And in Brazil its value is estimated at $1,395,000,000. Only — it has been suggested, that this diamond is a topaz, in which case the millions vanish.

No one is allowed to behold this diamond, which is still in the rough. And since the question of its nature is not tested, it may be presumed that the test is withheld for good reasons.

Of the value of the two other famous diamonds of Portugal there is no doubt. One weighs 215 carats, the other is flatter and weighs a little less. These beautiful stones were found by three men who were banished to the province of Minas Geraes, and who bought their freedom with them.

The crown of England is very rich in beautiful diamonds; its chief treasure is the famous Koh-i-noor, or "mountain of light."

The history of this stone is obscure, but, as already mentioned, it is believed to be the same gem as that described by Tavernier among the jewels of Aurengzebe. According to a Hindu legend it was worn by one of the heroes of the Indian epic poem the Mahabharata, and it would therefore have a history extending backward about 4000 years. Coming down to later times we find it in possession of Vikramaditya, rajah of Ujayin, 56 B.C., from whom it passed to his successors, the rajahs of Malwa, and latterly to the sultans of Delhi, when Malwa fell into their possession. Its later history is given by Mr. Hunt as follows:—"Nadir Shah, on his occupation of Delhi in 1739, compelled Mohammed Shah, the great-grandson of Aurengzebe, to give up to him everything of value that the imperial treasury possessed; and his biographer and secretary signifies a *peshkash* or present by Mohammed Shah to his conqueror of several mag-

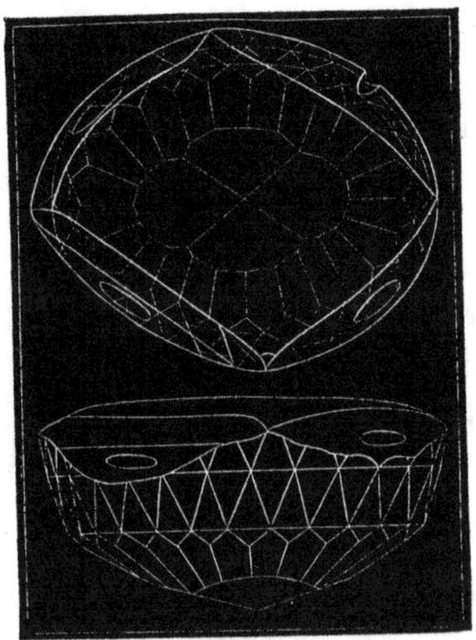

Fig. 40.—The Koh-i-noor before re-cutting.

nificent diamonds. According to the family and popular tradition Mohammed Shah wore the Koh-i-noor in front of his turban at his interview with his conqueror, who insisted in exchanging turbans in proof of his regard. However this might have been, we need have little doubt that the great diamond of Aurengzebe was in the possession of Mohammed Shah at the time of the Persian invasion; and if it was it most certainly changed masters, and became, as is universally asserted, the property of Nadir Shah, who is also said to have bestowed upon it the name of Koh-i-noor. After his death the diamond, which he had wrested from the unfortunate representative of the house of Timur, became the property of Ahmed Shah, the founder of the Abdali dynasty of Kabul, having been given to him, or more probably taken by him, from Shahrikh, the young son of Nadir. The jewel descended to the successors of Ahmed Shah, and when Mr. Elphinstone was at Peshawur was worn by Shah Shujah on his arm. When Shah Shujah was driven from Kabul he became the nominal guest and actual prisoner of Runjet Sing, who spared neither importunity nor menace, until, in 1813, he compelled the fugitive monarch to resign the precious gem, presenting him on the occasion, it is said, with a lakh and 25,000 rupees, or about $60,000. Runjet was highly elated by the acquisition of the diamond, and wore it as an armlet at all great festivals. When he was dying an attempt was made by persons about him to persuade him to make the diamond a present to Jaganath, and it is said that he intimated assent by an inclination of his head. The treasurer, however, whose charge it was, refused to give it up without better warrant, and Runjet dying before a written order could be signed by him, the Koh-i-noor was preserved for a while for his successors. It was occasionally worn by Rhurreuk Sing and Shu Sing. After the murder of the latter it remained in the Lahore treasury until the supercession of Dhulip Sing and the annexation of the Punjaub by the British government (1849), when the civil authorities took possession of the Lahore treasury, under the stipulations previously made that all the property of the state should be confiscated to the East India Company, in part payment of the debt due by the Lahore government, and of the expenses of the war; it was at the same time stipulated that the Koh-i-noor should be presented to the Queen of England. Such is the strange history of certainly one of the most extraordinary diamonds in the world. After the Company became possessed of the gem it was taken in charge by Lord Dalhousie, and sent by him to England in custody of two officers."

When the Koh-i-noor was brought to England it weighed $186\frac{1}{16}$ carats, and had the form shown in Fig. 40. It was exhibited in this state at the Great Exhibition of 1851, and was valued at about $700,000. At that time it was merely surface cut, and was also disfigured with several flaws, so that re-cutting seemed advisable; and it was decided to give it the form of the brilliant. The cutting was begun on July 16, 1852—the Duke of Wellington being the first person to place it on the cutting mill—and was finished Sept. 7, thus occupying in all thirty-eight days of twelve hours each. It had

Fig. 41.—The Koh-i-noor after being re-cut.

now the form represented in Fig. 41, its weight being reduced to 122¾ carats. In cutting it some parts were found to be very much harder than others. Though so much reduced in weight by this operation the Koh-i-noor has been much improved in brilliancy and effect.

Besides the Koh-i-noor, and a great number of

fine pearls, the crown of Queen Victoria contains 497 diamonds, of which the value is estimated at more than $372,000.

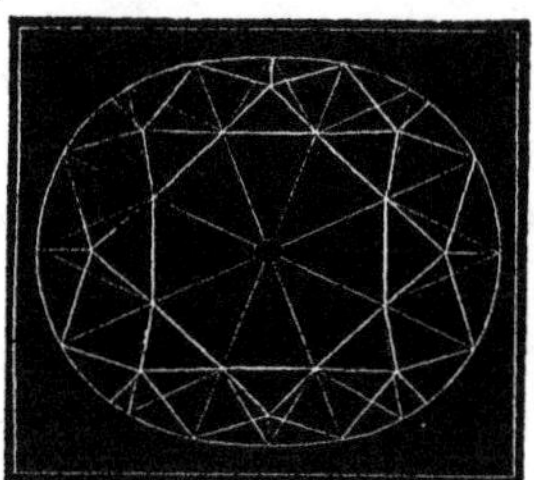

Fig. 42.—The Pigott.

Another well-known diamond is the Pigott, which was brought from the Indies by Lord Pigott. Its weight is 81½ carats. It was sold by lottery in 1801 for the sum of $139,500. Later it became the property of the Pasha of Egypt, who paid for it an equal sum. Fig. 42.

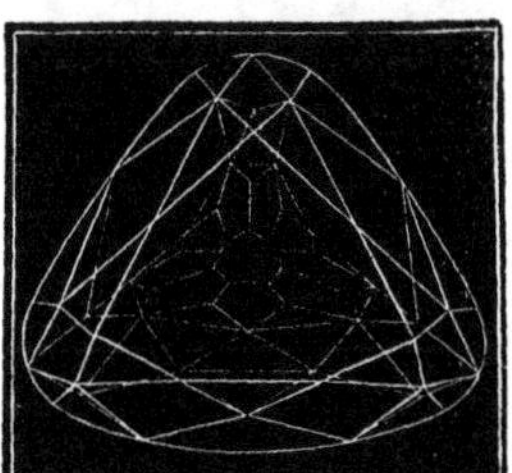

Fig. 43.—The Nassac.

The Nassâk or Nassac is a diamond of a triangular

form, with curved facettes, belonging to the Marquis of Westminster, who had it cut into its present form. It weighs 78⅝ carats, and is estimated at about $148,000.

The country that is most rich in diamonds at present is Russia.

Besides special collections of diamonds in the treasury of this empire, there are three crowns of which they form the sole jewels. The first, that of Ivan Alexiowitch, contains 881; that of Peter the Great, 847; and that of Catherine the Great, 2536.

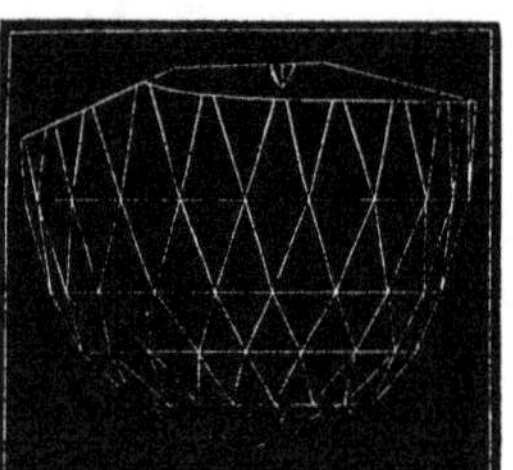

Fig. 44.—The Orlow.

Among the large diamonds in Russia the most remarkable is the Orlow. It weighs 193 carats. It has, as is shown by Fig. 44, the form of a half egg. It is one of the ornaments of the imperial sceptre.

This beautiful diamond was originally from India. It formed for a century and a half one of the eyes

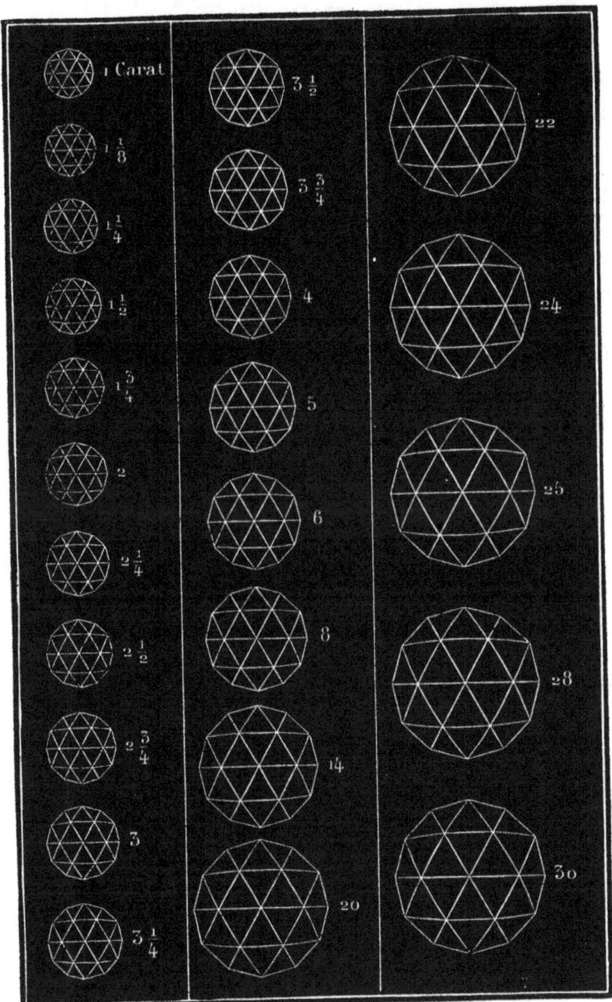

Fig. 45.—Surface of Roses compared to their Weight.

of the famous idol of Serringham in the temple of Brahma; the other eye was a diamond of the same order.

At the commencement of the eighteenth century the idea seized a French soldier of one of the French garrisons in India to steal the eyes of this celebrated idol. He pretended to be inspired with a wonderful zeal for the Hindu religion, and gained to that degree the confidence of the priests that

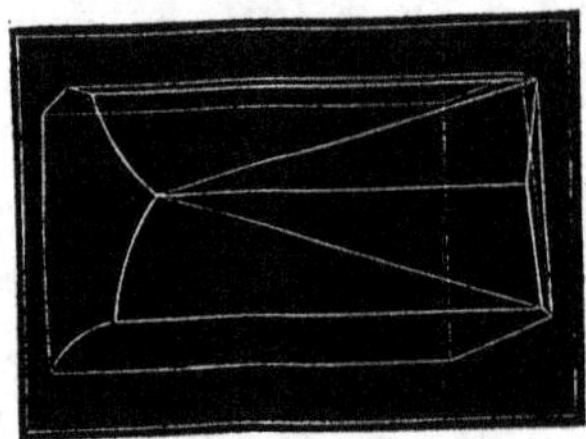

Fig. 46.—The Shah.

they confided to him the care of the temple. He chose his time, and one stormy night carried off one of the diamonds; the other could not be forced from the socket. He fled to Madras, where he sold the stolen treasure to a captain of the English navy for $9300. Conveyed to England it was bought for $55,800 by a Jewish merchant, who sometime after sold it to Catherine II. for $418,500, and a pension for life of $18,600.

It was this famous stone that suggested Wilkie Collins' novel "The Moonstone."

Another beautiful Russian diamond is called the Shah: it belonged once to the ancient monarchs of

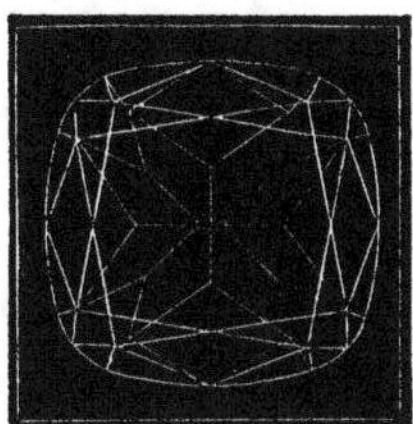

Fig. 47.—The Polar Star.

Persia. It is of very excellent water, and weighs 95 carats. Fig. 46 shows the peculiar form of this beautiful stone.

The third great Russian diamond is the "Moon of the Mountain." It was bought for 50,000 piastres

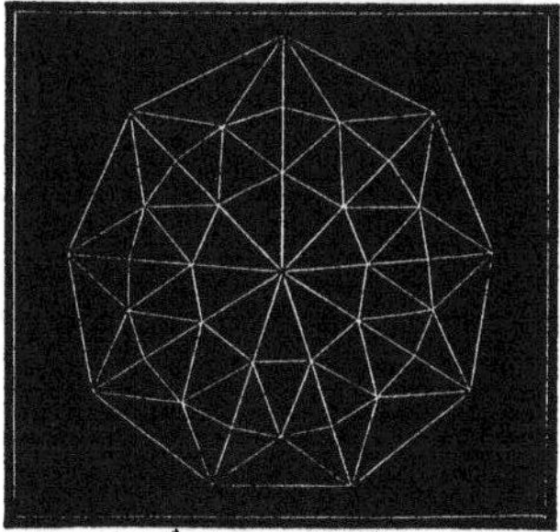

Fig. 48.—The Grand-duke of Tuscany.

of an Afghan chief by an Armenian merchant named Schafnass, who kept it for twelve years, and then sent it by his brother to Amsterdam, where, after a long negotiation, it was bought by Russia for $334,800 and a patent of nobility.

Russia possesses also a superb diamond, the Polar Star, cut as a brilliant, and weighing 40 carats. It belongs to the Princess Youssoupoff. Fig 47.

The finest diamond owned by Austria is the Grand-duke of Tuscany. It is a little yellow, and is cut to represent a star of nine rays. Fig. 48.

This diamond belonged to Charles the Bold, who lost it at the battle of Granson. Found by a soldier, it was sold by a Genoese merchant to Ludovic Sforza, duke of Milan. It became afterwards the property of Pope Julius II., who presented it to the Emperor of Austria. It weighs 139½ carats.

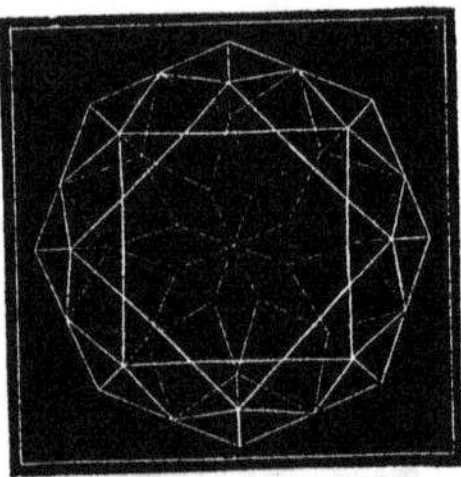

Fig. 49.—The Pasha of Egypt.

Egypt possesses a very beautiful brilliant of 40 carats, which bears the name of the Pasha of Egypt. It cost $136,200.

In Holland there is a diamond ot 36 carats, estimated at $48,360; and one in the treasury of Dresden that weighs 31¼ carats.

A *black diamond* was sold by M. Bapst to Louis XVIII. for the sum of $4464, but it was never delivered. Its colour was a very dark brown, and it had a remarkable lustre.

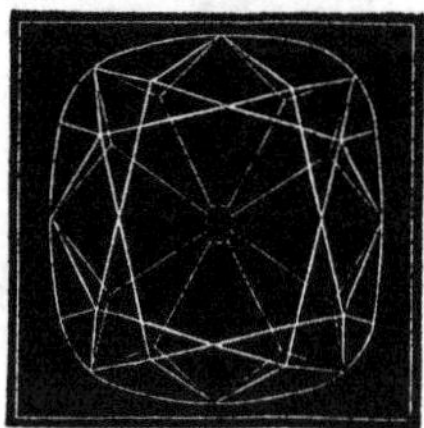

Fig. 50.—The Blue Diamond of Mr. Hope.

A precious stone without a rival is the *blue diamond* of Mr. Hope. Its weight is 44⅛ carats, and its colour is the blue of the most beautiful sapphire, added to an adamantine lustre of the utmost brilliancy. It was purchased for $83,700, but competent judges declare that it is worth more.

ENGRAVING UPON THE DIAMOND.

Notwithstanding its wonderful hardness, the diamond has been engraved.

In the Paris Exhibition of 1867, in the Italian section, an engraved diamond was exhibited. It

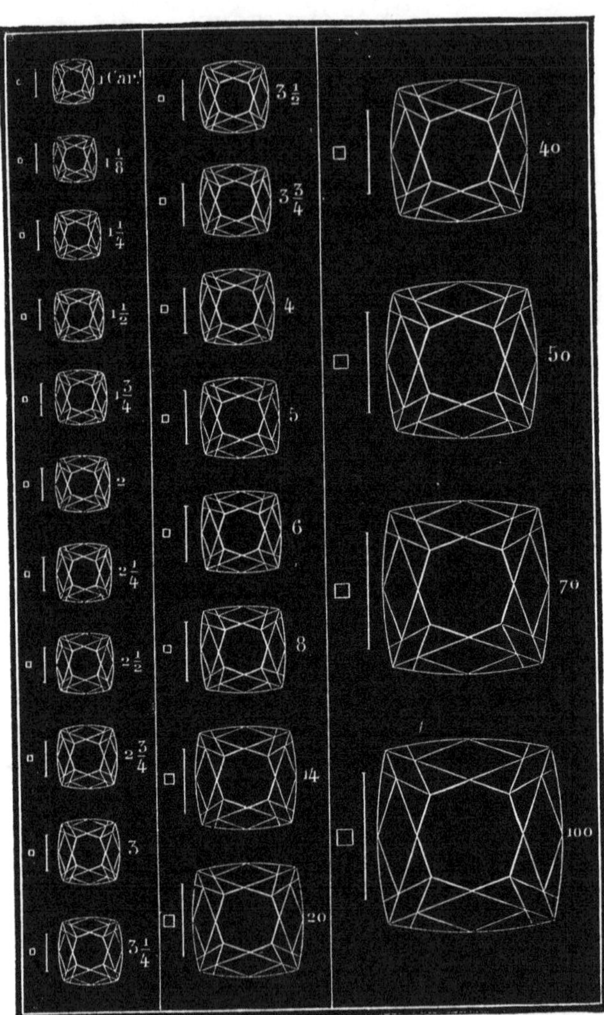

Fig. 51.—Surfaces of Brilliants compared to their weight. The vertical lines indicate the thickness of the stone.

was engraved in the sixteenth century by Jacopo or Como da Trezzo; and it was set in a unique cylindrical ring of gold, by aid of a movable collet upon pivots.

PART IV.

Sapphire. Ruby. Balas Ruby. Spinel Ruby. Topaz. Emerald. Beryl. Aquamarine. Cymophane. Turquoise.

" What wonder then, if fields and regions here
Breathe forth elixir pure, and rivers run
Potable gold, when with one virtuous touch
Th' arch-chemic Sun, so far from us remote,
Produces, with terrestrial humour mix'd
Here in the dark, so many precious things,
Of colour glorious, and effects so rare ? "

Every one knows that common substance called *clay*, which is so easily mixed into a paste with water. But every one does not consider perhaps what an important part in agriculture and industry this familiar substance performs.

All soils that are of value for the production of vegetables contain clay. The principal element of this substance—*alumina*—is necessary to the development of plants; and its presence is necessary to retain the humidity of soil that is indispensable to vegetable life.

To indicate the importance of clay in the industrial world it is only necessary to say that tiles, bricks, pottery, from the coarsest kind to the finest

Sèvres ware, are almost exclusively formed of this substance.

And what is clay?

To answer this question categorically is impossible, because there are comprehended under that name a multitude of mixtures, whose composition is extremely variable; but the only fact important for us to know here is that the principal constituent element of clay is alumina.

In these modern times industry has been enriched by an important conquest, *aluminium*, that new metal which, whether used alone or in combination with other metals, lends itself with complete success to the manifold wants of the industrial arts. It is a discovery and creation for which our epoch is indebted to the French chemist M. Henri Sainte-Claire Deville.

If this metal is combined with the oxygen of the air, the metal disappears, and is transformed into the rust of aluminium; exactly as the brilliant and metallic iron is transformed into iron rust under the same conditions; only that aluminium rust is white instead of red. This white rust is pure alumina.

Now this alumina exists in a prodigious quantity, not only in vegetable mould, but also in a large portion of the rocks of our globe. Generally it is mixed with iron rust, which gives it a red colour, or it may be with other substances; but it now and then occurs in absolute purity; and it is always possible to extract pure alumina from any kind of clay.

If we ask now what is the composition of the precious stones whose names figure at the head of this chapter, we are answered—they are formed of alumina nearly pure. Besides this they contain only some faint traces of foreign matters, generally of the oxide of iron.

Notwithstanding the minute quantities, these foreign matters are very important, because it is to their union with alumina that the precious stones we are considering owe their remarkable colour, and consequently a great part of their commercial value.

But if the ruby, the sapphire, and kindred gems, are formed almost exclusively of alumina, we must hasten to add that this alumina is *crystallized*, for in this fact is comprehended the cause of the enormous distance which separates the alumina of the soil around us from the alumina of which precious stones are composed.

CORUNDUM.

Modern mineralogists have given the single name *corundum* to all the minerals consisting of crystallized alumina almost pure, without regard to the colour of these minerals.

Corundum comprehends three varieties: the hyaline corundum, the laminated corundum, and the granular corundum. The first variety comprehends the precious stones.

The primitive form of the crystals of corundum is the six-sided prism (Fig. 52), but the most general form of the hyaline corundum is the dodecahedron (Fig. 53), with faces formed of isosceles triangles.

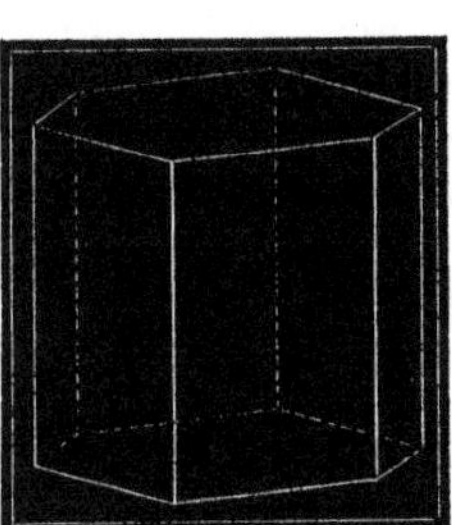

Fig. 52.—Primitive form of Corundum.

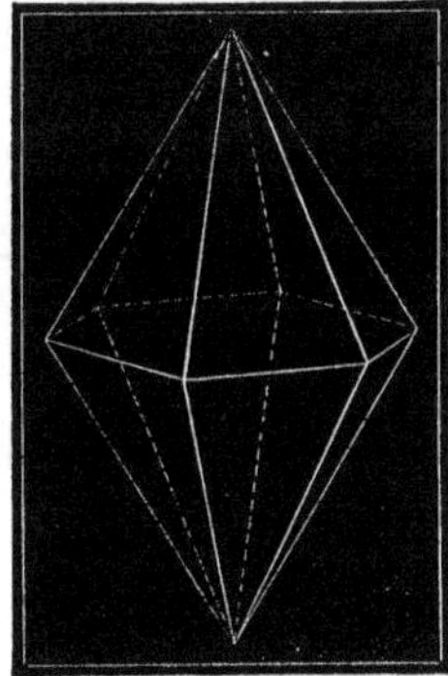

Fig. 53.—Most common form of the Corundum.

Nearly all the hyaline corundums susceptible of being employed in jewelry are brought from Pegu. The price of these stones is very high. It is not a rare occurrence for the price of the ruby to exceed that of the diamond. At an auction of precious stones from the cabinet of M. Drée a very beautiful diamond of 8 grains (2 carats) was sold for $148, while a ruby of the same weight brought $186. At the same sale the price of a ruby of 10 grains reached $2604. The value of the ruby and that of precious stones generally varies with their richness of tone.

When the corundum is perfectly colourless it possesses a brilliancy so vivid that in some circumstances it may pass for a diamond. It may be distinguished from the latter by its inferior hardness, its smaller specific gravity (3·5, while that of the diamond is 3·9), and by having double refraction.

According to the tints which the corundum possesses, it bears different names, and represents variable values.

Names of the corundums according to their colour:—

White Sapphire,	Colourless.
Oriental Ruby,	Crimson red
Oriental Ruby (variety),	Rose red.
Oriental Sapphire,	Azure blue.
Indigo Sapphire,	Indigo blue.
Oriental Amethyst,	Violet.
Oriental Topaz,	Yellow.
Oriental Emerald,	Green.

THE RUBY.

There exists but one true ruby, the oriental ruby.

The spinel ruby and the balas ruby must be carefully distinguished from this valuable gem, as neither in nature nor composition do they resemble the oriental ruby.

"The oriental ruby," says Babinet, "ranks first for price and beauty among all coloured stones. When its colour is of good quality it has the vivid tint of arterial blood (a tint called 'pigeon's blood' in commerce), or of the very centre of the red ray in the solar spectrum. It is the perfect red of the painter's palette, without any mixture of violet or of orange. Several of the reds in the stained glass of our ancient cathedrals, when the daylight pours through them, give an idea of this brilliant colour.

"The ruby is extremely hard; and after the sapphire, which surpasses it a little in this respect, it is the hardest of precious stones, always excepting the diamond, to which nothing can compare. M. Charles Achard, the highest authority in France in all that concerns the traffic in coloured stones, remarks that weight has not the same effect in their case as in that of the diamond. Every diamond, from the very smallest specimen upwards, has its value like gold or silver, according to weight; but in the case of rubies and other gems the little specimens have hardly any value; and these stones only begin to be appreciated at the moment when their weight withdraws them from the common ruck, and assures at once their rarity and high price. When a perfect ruby of 5 carats enters the market a price will be offered for it double the price of a perfect diamond of the same weight; and if a ruby reaches the weight of 10 carats it will bring triple the price of a diamond of the same weight (from three to four thousand dollars).

"I have seen many collections of amateurs, visited and consulted many lapidaries, and everyone admits that a perfect ruby is the most rare of all the productions of nature. The tint of the ruby is as admirable by artificial light as by the light of day."

The precious stone called the carbuncle by the ancients is the same as our modern ruby.

The most fantastic qualities were formerly ascribed to these wonderful stones. The carbuncle served to furnish light to certain great serpents or dragons when old age had enfeebled their eyes; they constantly carried these magical stones between their teeth, only dropping them when it was necessary to eat and to drink. And according to St. Epiphanius the carbuncle has not only the property of shining brilliantly in darkness, but its light is of a nature so extraordinary that nothing can arrest it; so that it shines, for instance, through vestments with undiminished fire.

At the same time that it is averred that the carbuncle of the ancients included our oriental ruby, it is equally certain that this name was applied to all red stones—oriental ruby, spinel ruby, garnets, &c. —in the same indiscriminate manner as the East Indians apply the name ruby to all coloured precious stones.

When Pegu, that fatherland of rubies, was annexed in 1852 to the English possessions, it was believed that Europe would receive at least a part of the rubies that had been for so many centuries locked up in that country. That hope has been completely disappointed. It is not even certain that the mines there continue to be worked. It would seem also that the regions where rubies exist are extremely dangerous to approach on account of lions, tigers, and serpents. To be sure, it is very probable that merchants in rubies designedly exaggerate these dangers to delay competition; but it is certain that this part of Asia is very little known, and the known condition of the island of Borneo seems to justify the opinion.

SPINEL RUBY AND BALAS RUBY.

In connection with the oriental ruby two other productions of quite a different nature must be described, namely, the spinel ruby and the balas ruby.

The first is generally a very vivid poppy red;

the second of a violet rose, or a vinegar rose; but there is no absolute rule for their colour, since Pegu furnishes white and violet-white spinels; and specimens have been brought from Aker in Sudermania which are of a bluish gray.

Spinels are brought also from Ceylon and other oriental countries; everywhere they are found in the beds of torrents, in the midst of alluvial deposits.

The primitive form of the crystals of spinel ruby is octahedral, like that of the diamond; this characteristic suffices to distinguish immediately the spinel or balas ruby from the oriental ruby, since the crystals of the latter present the form of six-sided prisms.

The composition of the spinel ruby and balas ruby differ essentially from that of the oriental ruby, the latter being a corundum formed nearly exclusively of alumina, while in the former only 70 parts in 100 are alumina, and the remainder chiefly magnesia. The colour, moreover, is in part due to the oxide of chromium, a substance of which the oriental ruby does not contain the slightest trace.

In a scientific point of view the balas ruby does not differ from the spinel; and many special works confound the two completely. But in commerce the stone called Balas has a value very much below that of the spinel.

In the inventory of the crown jewels of France the price of balas rubies is four or five times less than that of spinels.

CELEBRATED RUBIES.

The largest ruby known is one mentioned by Chardin as having been engraved with the name of Sheik Sephy.

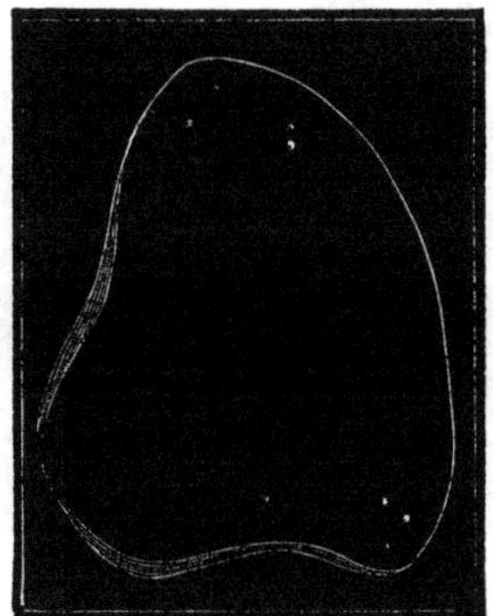

Fig. 54.—King of Persia's Ruby.

Tavernier gives a figure of another celebrated ruby in the possession of the King of Persia: it is reproduced in Fig. 54. Its weight was 175 carats.

A third, belonging to the King of Visapur, had the figure and dimensions of Fig. 55. It was cut, as will be seen, *en cabochon*, and it had been bought in 1653 for nearly $13,866.

A fourth, seen by Tavernier in India, is represented by Fig. 56.

According to the judgment of Tavernier it was of secondary beauty; yet this celebrated traveller offered $11,160 to the diamond merchant who possessed it, but could not obtain it at that price.

A ruby possessed by Gustavus Adolphus, and presented by him to the Czarina in 1777, at the

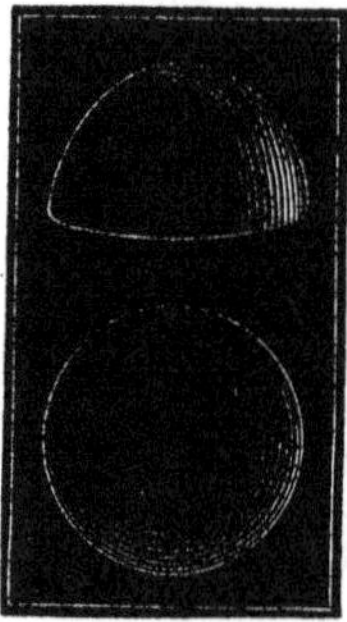

Fig. 55.—Ruby of the King of Visapur.

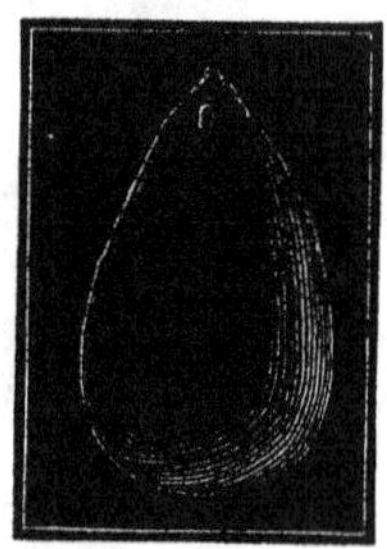

Fig. 56.—Indian Ruby.

time of his journey to St. Petersburg, was the size of a small hen's egg.

A ruby in the French crown, adorning the order of the golden fleece, is in the form of a dragon.

Finally, it is seen from the inventory of 1791 that France then possessed eighty-one oriental rubies, estimated at $6138.

In England the ruby is especially prized; and some beautiful and very valuable stones are in the hands of the nobility. In America it is less highly estimated.

ENGRAVING UPON RUBIES.

The ancients seldom engraved the ruby. Pliny ascribes this fact to the singular reason that seals made of this stone *carried away the wax.*

The excessive hardness of the ruby, its costliness, and the great rarity of specimens proper for engraving are, without doubt, the true reasons which prevented the ancients from engraving it; the impossibility, moreover, of polishing the cavities made in this substance may have occasioned the fault which Pliny has ascribed to ruby signets.

In the Odescalchi museum the design of an engraved ruby represents Ceres standing with an ear of corn in her hand.

Another engraved ruby represents a bearded head, supposed to be that of a Greek philosopher. This ruby is cut in the shape of a heart, and formed a part of the collection of the Duke of Orleans.

Both these engraved rubies are spinel rubies.

THE SAPPHIRE.

The word *sapphire* is derived from the Syriac *saphilah,* a name which indicates the same stone in this Eastern tongue.

In commerce there are four different stones that bear the name of sapphire:—

Oriental Sapphire.	Sapphire of Puy.
Brazilian Sapphire.	Water Sapphire.

The three first are corundums, and consequently true sapphires. The last is a coloured quartz, and a stone of but trifling value.

The oriental sapphire has been known from earliest antiquity. It was one of the precious stones that had place in the breastplate of Aaron. To the ancients it was the gem of gems, the sacred stone *par excellence.* The Greeks dedicated it to Apollo.

The first sapphires that reached Europe came from Arabia; later they were imported from Persia. At the present day they are found principally in Arabia and the Brazils; and the productions of both these countries are called oriental sapphires.

There are certain sapphires, generally of a pale colour, which, when examined under the microscope, exhibit thread-like shafts directed towards the faces of the six-sided prism; these threads are produced by foreign substances, or by vacuities left among the molecules at the moment of their crystallization. The light reflected upon them forms a star of six rays, extremely beautiful and remarkable. Sapphires of this kind are called *asteria sapphires,* or *star sapphires.*

The orientals have a deep veneration for the star sapphire; and M. D'Abbadie, in his travels in Africa, often commanded the respect of the natives by allowing a stone of this kind, which he always carried with him, to exhibit its magical beauty to their astonished eyes.

A stone of a yellow-green tint, exhibiting a similar phenomenon, is brought from Ceylon. It is called the *Cat's Eye.* Threads of white asbestos are inclosed within it, and the light is reflected from these in an intense manner. When this stone is cut *en cabochon,* a white band of light is seen floating in its interior, that changes position as the gem is moved before the eye.

The sapphire of Puy is found in the rivulets of Expilly. Its colour varies from the deepest to the palest blue; sometimes it passes to a reddish blue, or even to a yellowish green. Its composition is not always homogeneous; and the specimens which display the finest water are those in which the tint verges upon green. They are found in ferruginous sand produced by decomposition of basaltic rocks.

Fig. 57 is a view of the mountain of Expilly, where the sapphires of Puy are found.

Among the celebrated sapphires we must mention above all that which figured in the famous "affair of the necklace."

Found in Bengal by a poor man who sold wooden

spoons, it was brought to Europe, and bought by the house of Raspoli at Rome. Later it became the property of a German prince, who sold it to Perret, a Parisian jeweller, for $31,620. This beautiful stone, without blemish or faults of any kind, weighed 133⅙ carats. It formed afterwards part of the riches of the Museum of Natural History at Paris.

This museum possesses another sapphire of exquisite beauty and exceptional size. It is oval, and measures two inches by one and a half.

A very beautiful star sapphire belongs to one of the merchant princes of New York; and in England, among the jewels of Miss Burdett Coutts, are two magnificent sapphires estimated at $139,500.

In the Hope collection—among several fine specimens of this gem—is a stone called the "Marvellous Sapphire," which is blue by day and amethystine at night. This gem is said to have afforded the foundation of one of Madame de Genlis' stories.

ENGRAVED SAPPHIRES.

The ancients engraved the sapphire notwithstanding its extreme hardness.

There is a beautiful sapphire among the crown jewels of Russia representing a female figure enveloped in drapery. The stone is of two tints, and

Fig. 57.—View of the Mountain of Expilly, Central France.

the artist has skilfully used the dark tint for the woman and the light tint for the drapery. This gem formed part of the collection of the Duke of Orleans.

The cabinet of France possesses in sapphire a very remarkable intaglio representing the Emperor Pertinax.

The marvel of this kind is an engraving by Cneïus representing the profile of a young Hercules. It is in the Strozzi Cabinet at Rome.

THE TOPAZ.

The topaz, like its kindred precious stones, is divided into the occidental and the oriental.

The oriental topaz should be in every respect carefully distinguished, because it is the only variety which is composed of alumina nearly pure. The others contain no more than 57 or 58 parts to 100 of this substance.

The topaz of the moderns is the chrysolite of the ancients. It is a corundum coloured by a slight quantity of the oxide of iron to a beautiful golden yellow. The topaz was originally found, as Pliny informs us, upon an island in the Red Sea, which, being often surrounded by fog, was so difficult to find that the mariners named it *Topaza* (Gr. *topazein*, to guess).

This stone is now very rare; and when to the fineness of its quality it joins a soft clear colour with a satin-like lustre, it acquires a considerable value. But the topaz, however perfect, never reaches the price of a ruby or a sapphire, or even a fine emerald of equal dimensions.

Occidental Topaz.—Stones thus designated are not corundums. They are of a more complex composition; and the analysis of specimens brought from different localities proves that occidental topazes are not identical. They have for a long time been divided into four varieties:—

Brazilian Topaz.	Mexican Topaz.
Saxon Topaz.	Siberian Topaz.

It should be remarked, however, that while the proportions of the elements differ in each of these varieties, their nature is the same. The occidental topaz is in all cases formed of alumina, silica, and fluoric acid. The presence of this last substance, found in no other precious stone, characterizes perfectly the genus topaz in respect to chemical composition.

The primitive type of crystals of topaz is the right rhomboidal prism (Fig. 58).

Certain modifications occur in the form of these crystals, which, joined to their colour, enable a person to decide as to which of the varieties any topaz in question belongs.

The Saxon topaz generally occurs in the form of a rhomboidal prism with a base; and its colour varies from an orange yellow to a straw yellow.

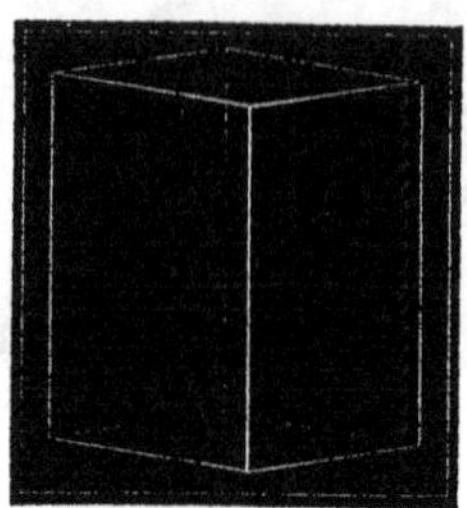

Fig. 58.—Type of Crystal of Topaz.

The Brazilian topaz exhibits most frequently a rhomboidal prism surmounted by a four-faced pyra-

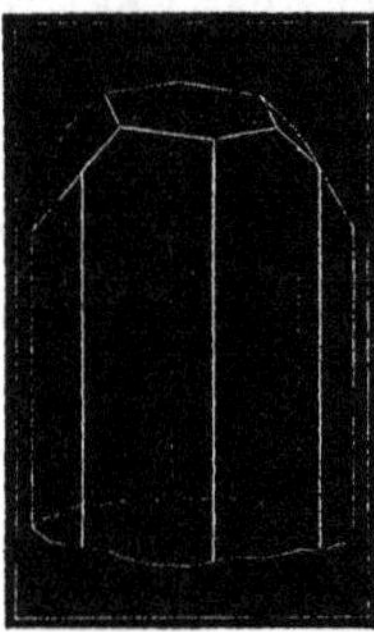

Fig. 59.—Saxon Topaz.

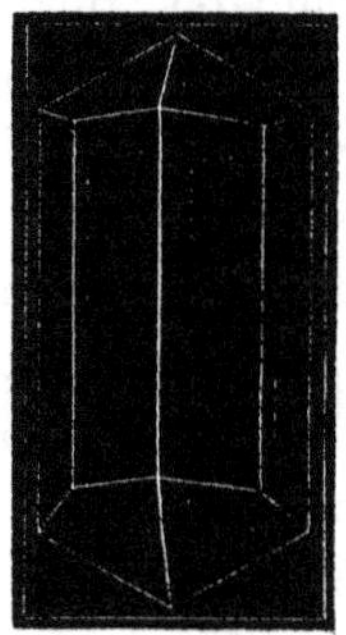

Fig. 60.—Brazilian Topaz.

mid, and its colour includes all the shades from orange yellow to wine yellow.

The Siberian topaz is nearly always found in rhomboidal prisms, terminated by a ditetragonal pyramid; it is of a pale blue or green cast of colour, and sometimes occurs colourless, when it is much prized. Although in form of crystallization these Siberian minerals are really topazes, they approach very nearly by their tint and transparency to the aquamarine.

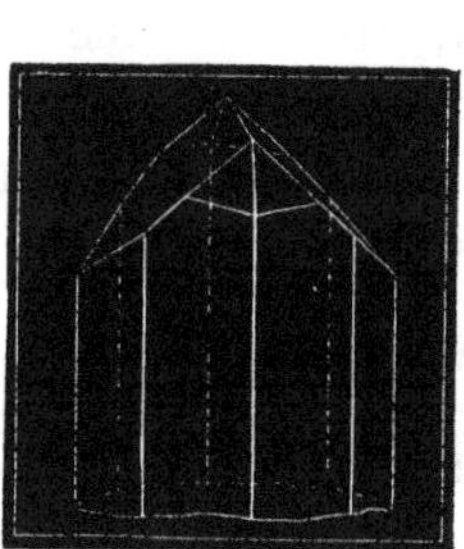

Fig. 61.—Siberian Topaz.

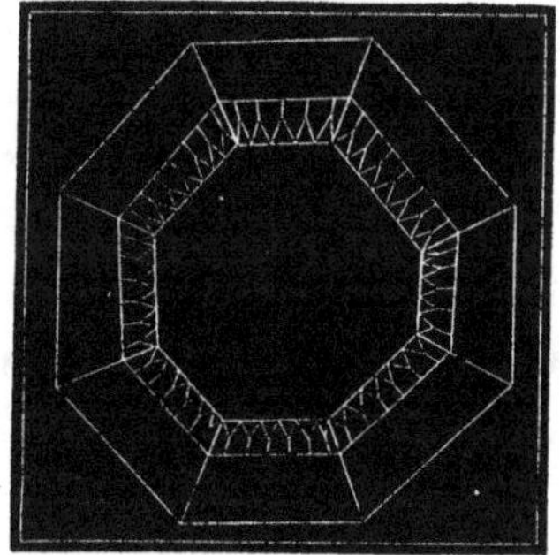

Fig. 62.—Topaz of the Grand Mogul.

A finely polished topaz belonging to the Grand Mogul was purchased at Goa for $50,500. It weighed 157¼ carats, and was cut in the form represented by Fig. 62.

ENGRAVING UPON THE TOPAZ.

It was for a long time believed that the ancients never engraved this gem; but Caire mentions a topaz which he had had in his own possession weighing 29 carats, and engraved in Arabic with the motto, "*No one accomplishes but God.*" It was probably an amulet, such as are worn by orientals of the present day, and which are called by the Arabs *gri-gri.*

Another celebrated engraved topaz represents Philip II. and Don Carlos. It is a white topaz, engraved by Jacopo da Trezzo.

The house of Orleans had a very beautiful octagonal topaz engraved with a Mercury; and in Turin, in the Generosio collection, was a celebrated topaz intaglio, representing Victory enthroned in a chariot.

THE AMETHYST.

The oriental amethyst is a rare substance of magnificent lustre, and of a violet colour slightly tinted with red.

The amethyst was the ninth stone in the breastplate of Aaron; and in modern times it is the sacred stone which ornaments the cross and the pastoral ring of Catholic bishops.

In the inventory of the crown jewels of France, 1791, three superb oriental amethysts are mentioned, one of which weighed $13\frac{8}{16}$ carats, and was valued at $1116.

But the greater part of the amethysts of commerce

are occidental amethysts. As their composition and value have nothing in common with the oriental amethyst they will be described elsewhere.

ENGRAVING UPON THE AMETHYST.

Ancient engravings upon amethyst are numerous. That which has been chosen as an example (Fig. 63) represents Antonia, the daughter of Mark Antony, and the wife of Drusus, a beautiful

Fig. 63.—Antonia, wife of Drusus.

princess, who, to use the touching language of Lenormant, "embodied in herself all the glory and the sorrow of her time." She is represented as the goddess Ceres, and carries a horn of plenty. In the National Library of France there is a magnificent work in amethyst, a profile (supposed to be Maecenas at an advanced age) engraved by Dioscorides, one of the four celebrated engravers mentioned by Pliny.

Among the finest gems of the Pulsky collection is the head of a Syrian king upon a pale tinted amethyst, engraved with the artist's name ΝΕΑΡΚΗΣ

EMERALD, BERYL, AQUAMARINE.

These three substances are, in a scientific point of view, very nearly identical; but in commerce the value of the emerald is infinitely greater than that of the beryl and aquamarine.

The emerald, when it possesses a green tint of a beautiful quality, and when it is entirely hyaline, is one of the most rare and precious of gems. On the contrary, when it appears in semi-transparent crystals of a watery green, it is quite common; indeed there are few granitic mountains where it has not been observed.

The colour so remarkable in the emerald is due to a pretty large quantity, 8 to 9 parts in 100, of oxide of chromium.

The fundamental form of crystals of emerald is the regular six-sided prism. As the side of the base nearly always equals the height, the faces of emerald crystals vary very little from a square.

Another form which frequently occurs is the twelve-sided prism, which is derived directly from the primitive form by the modification of the six vertical edges.

Like the other corundums the emerald is formed chiefly of alumina, but it has a peculiarity which renders it interesting to the chemist, since it contains a considerable proportion, 12 to 15 parts in 100, of a rare body, *glucina*, the discovery of which is due to the illustrious chemist Vauquelin.

It was for a long time believed that emeralds were always found in connection with granitic rocks;

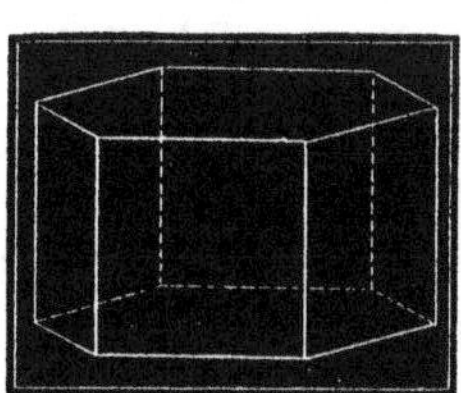

Fig. 64.—Fundamental Form of Emerald Crystals.

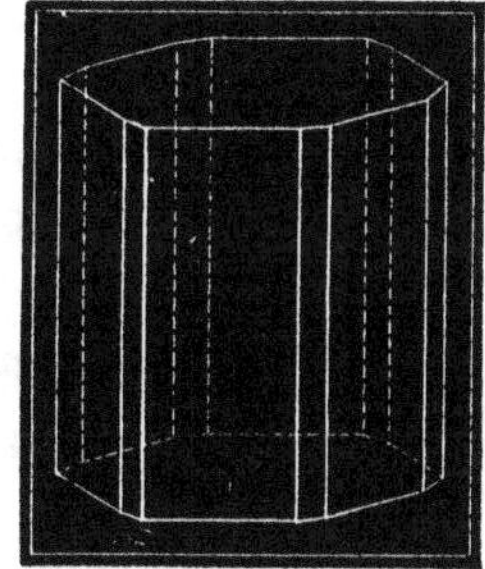

Fig. 65.—Very common Form of Emerald Crystals.

but in 1848 M. Léwy, in the course of his travels in New Grenada, discovered that this opinion was erroneous.

M. Léwy has shown in fact that the most beautiful specimens, those of the mine of Mouza, so far from existing in crystalline rocks, exist, on the contrary, in the best defined secondary formations—in that division of the cretaceous formation to which geologists have given the name of the neocomian. The fossils brought home by M. Léwy leave no room for doubt on this subject.

Since the publication of the discovery of M. Léwy, MM. Nicaize and Montigny have found in the valley of the Harrach, in the province of Constantine (Algeria), a bed of emeralds, appertaining, like that of America, to the cretaceous formation.

BERYL AND AQUAMARINE.

The beryl and the aquamarine have the general composition and constitution of the emerald; but they differ from it in the absence of the oxide of chromium, which is in them replaced by the oxide of iron. The colour remains the same, but it is much feebler and less pure than in true emeralds.

Beryl.—Among lapidaries and dealers in precious stones the beryl and the aquamarine constitute a well-defined group, altogether distinct from the emerald. With them the beryl is the oriental species of this group, and the aquamarine the occidental.

For a long time the beryl was only known in India; afterwards it was met with in Arabia; and still later remarkable fragments of it were found in Russia, at Beresof, and in the environs of Lake Bolchoi.

Aquamarine.—The aquamarine is a stone of but trifling value, and yet it possesses a quality which should have prevented it from falling into its present low estimate; *it does not lose its brilliancy in artificial lights.*

"It is a curious spectacle," says Babinet, "to see a magnificent blue sapphire lose in the night all its glories, when a poor trinket of aquamarine not only retains all its effect, but even seems to gain brilliancy. The English are as fond of the aquamarine as the Spanish are of the topaz."

The greater part of the aquamarines of commerce are furnished by Brazil. They are brought to Europe completely cut, and are sold by weight, but with extreme variations, since large and beautiful specimens are valued at from $75 to $95 the ounce, while the small ones hardly bring $5.

Formerly the aquamarine was very abundant in Daouria, upon the frontiers of China, whence the Russian merchants took them in exchange for furs. They are now found in Siberia, the Ural Mountains, the Altai Mountains, &c.

The emerald, so highly esteemed in our day, was not less valued by the ancients. Pliny describes it in the following terms:—

"There is no colour so pleasing to the eye as that of the emerald. Whoever delights in the verdure of herb and leaf must enjoy infinitely more the contemplation of emeralds, for no verdure can compare to theirs. They are the only stones that charm the eye without wearying it. Even when the eyes are fatigued by having looked too continuously on anything, the sight of an emerald soothes and strengthens them. Lapidaries can find nothing more refreshing for their tired eyes than the soft greenness of this stone. It loses its lustre neither in sun nor in shade, nor in artificial lights. It shines continually with the same soft glow."

The emerald is mentioned several times in our translation of the Bible, but it is not certain that the word so translated really meant our emerald.

Among precious stones there is not one that has formed the basis of such great exaggerations as the emerald.

It is Herodotus who first describes those gigantic emeralds of which Theophrastus, Appian, and Pliny make later mention.

Theophrastus relates that in the books of the Egyptians it was stated that a king of Babylon had sent to one of their kings an emerald four cubits long and three thick; and that there was in Egypt, in a temple of Jupiter, an obelisk made of four emeralds, which nevertheless was forty cubits long, four cubits thick at some places, and two in others. He adds, also, that at the time when he wrote, there was yet to be seen at Tyre, in the temple of Hercules, an upright column, made of a single emerald. Appian, too, describes a colossal statue of Serapis, of the height of nine cubits, carved out of a single emerald.

It is evident that these descriptions do not apply to our modern emerald. The productions they refer to were probably jasper and malachite; and, above all, vitreous masses artificially coloured by metallic oxides.

REMARKABLE BERYLS AND AQUAMARINES.

The finest beryl known is in the collection of Mr. Hope. It weighs nearly 6½ ounces, and cost $2325. It came from the mine of Cangayum, in the district of Coimbatoor, in the East Indies.

A magnificent beryl surmounts the globe in the royal crown of England. It is perfectly clear, and of a lovely colour. It is cut in an oval form, and is $2\frac{1}{10}$ inches long, 1½ in width, and $1\frac{1}{5}$ in depth.

A celebrated aquamarine adorned the tiara of Pope Julius II. It measured $2\frac{1}{10}$ inches in length, and $2\frac{2}{5}$ in thickness. Notwithstanding a slight flaw, it was considered by amateurs a very remarkable gem.

Caire mentions an aquamarine which he had seen in London that weighed when cut 250 carats, and was valued by its possessor at $465.

In 1827, in the town of Mouzinskaïa in Russia, a superb specimen of aquamarine was found, valued, we are seriously told by the Russians, at $111,600.

ENGRAVING UPON AQUAMARINE.

A considerable number of both modern and ancient engravings are executed upon this stone. The gem represented in Fig. 66 is a part of the

Fig. 66.—Julia, daughter of Titus.

collection of the National Library of France. It is the head of Julia, the daughter of Titus, and is signed by the artist Evodus. It was mounted originally with sapphires and pearls, and formed part of the decorations of a reliquary belonging to the abbey of St. Denis.

ENGRAVING UPON THE EMERALD.

The brittle texture of the emerald prevented it from being a favourite with engravers, consequently there are few engraved emeralds.

There is a description of a beautiful composition executed in the middle ages upon this stone. It represented the soul led away by the pleasures.

CYMOPHANE.

The cymophane is formed like the emerald, of alumina and glucina.

The cymophane of modern mineralogists is the oriental chrysolite, the chrysopal, and the chrysoberyl of the lapidaries. It is remarkable for its lively brilliancy, its polish, similar to that of the sapphire, and its warm gay tint. But its celebrity arises from its unique property of displaying blue reflections, with a milky tint that seems floating in its interior. This circumstance originated the name given to it by Haüy, which signifies *floating light.*

Crystals of cymophane are usually found in alluvial soils; in Ceylon and Brazil they occur in the same sands that furnish crystals of topaz, corundum, &c.—sands formed by the disintegration of ancient rocks. Fine specimens of cymophane have recently been found in Connecticut and in the Ural Mountains.

THE TURQUOISE.

There are two species of oriental turquoise, the *old rock* and the *new rock;* and there is also an occidental turquoise.

The terms *old rock* and *new rock* were applied to the turquoise in Persia. "The mine of turquoise," says Tavernier, "which furnishes the most beautiful stones, is three days' journey from Meshed, turning to the north-west after passing the large town of Nishabourg; it is the old rock. The other, which is five days' journey, was discovered and worked more recently; it furnishes turquoises of a whitish blue, and almost valueless; it is the new rock."

When Tavernier travelled in the East the King of Persia had already for a long time reserved for himself all the products of the old rock. He had ornaments made of them, which he presented to princes and kings.

When the embassy was sent by the King of Persia to Louis XIV., among the many rich presents conveyed to the French monarch were a large quantity of turquoises. But all those who saw them were unanimous in deciding that they were noways remarkable, and by no means answered the idea that had prevailed in Europe, of the much vaunted turquoises of the old rock. Perhaps the mine was already more or less exhausted.

Oriental Turquoise.—This is another aluminous stone; but alumina forms hardly more than half of its composition.

The blue colour, so characteristic of the turquoise, is due, in great part at least, to a combination of phosphoric acid, copper, and iron, and probably also to water, of which it contains 18 or 19 parts in 100.

The turquoise harmonizes well with diamonds and pearls, and is frequently employed in jewelry. It is consequently an object of some commercial consideration; but as it is pretty abundant it does not reach a high price, unless in specimens of a very unusual size.

At the sale of M. Drée's cabinet, a turquoise of the old rock, measuring ·47 inch by ·43 inch, was sold for $93; and as an example of the wide difference between the turquoises of the old and the new rock, there was sold at the same sale, for $22·50, a turquoise of the new rock, ·39 inch by ·37 inch, of the most beautiful sky-blue tint.

The turquoise is the stone that the orientals employ most frequently for amulets. Sentences are frequently engraved upon them, and generally quoted from the Koran.

Occidental Turquoise.—The occidental turquoise

is a substance altogether special in its composition, and above all in its organic origin.

It is, in point of fact, a fossil ivory, produced from the teeth of a past race of animals, brought accidentally in contact with substances containing copper, and which has absorbed a sufficient quantity of them to colour the entire mass with a cerulean hue more or less deep.

ENGRAVING UPON THE TURQUOISE.

The low degree of hardness possessed by the turquoise probably deterred the ancients from often engraving on this stone, or, it may be, these specimens of antiquity have not been sufficiently durable to reach our time. In either case, there are very few engraved turquoises known. Caire, however, cites a few.

In the Genevosio collection there is an amulet, convex on one side and flat on the other, showing upon one side an engraving of a veiled Diana holding two branches in her hands, upon the other a sort of sistrum, a star, and a bee: Greek letters are inscribed upon both faces.

The cabinet of the Duke of Orleans contained two engraved turquoises; one representing Diana, with her quiver upon her shoulder; and the other, the elder Faustina.

A turquoise in the gallery of Florence, nearly as

large as a small billiard ball, is engraved with a head which is possibly that of Cæsar, but more probably of Tiberius.

The group which we have just examined comprehends a certain number of precious stones that may be easily confounded with each other, or with certain other gems of which we have yet to speak.

As will be seen from the table at the end of the book, in which are briefly stated the general characters of precious stones, it is almost always possible to distinguish with tolerable facility those that at first sight might be confounded.

Thus, the transparent and colourless corundum resembles the diamond, the aquamarine, the colourless spinel, and the quartz.

Now the corundum has double refraction, and the diamond simple refraction; accordingly nothing else is necessary than to look at the flame of a candle through the doubtful stone, in the manner pointed out in Chapter i.

The specific gravity of the corundum—3·9—enables us to distinguish it at once from quartz, of which the specific gravity is only 2·65, and from the emerald, which has a specific gravity of about 2·67. The white spinel, which, like the diamond, possesses simple refraction, will be distinguished from the corundum by the same optical test.

The red-coloured corundum may be confounded with the red spinel, the red tourmaline, and the burnt topaz.

The optical distinction applicable to the colourless spinel is equally so to the coloured spinel. The tourmaline and burnt topaz, again, may be easily distinguished from the corundum by their specific gravities alone—that of the tourmaline being 3·07, that of the topaz 2·65.

The oriental sapphire may be mistaken for the water sapphire or the blue emerald; the green corundum for the emerald of Bogota; the yellow corundum for the yellow topaz, the yellow quartz, the cymophane, and the zircon. The occidental amethyst, lastly, may be confounded with the oriental amethyst.

In all these cases the specific gravities are often sufficient, and when employed in conjunction with the other characters indicated in the general table they always enable us to decide with certainty.

PART V.

Quartz. Occidental Topaz. Smoky Topaz, or Alençon Diamond. Water Sapphire. False Emerald. Bohemian or Brazilian Ruby. Hyacinthe of Compostella. Iris. Aventurine. Opal. Hydrophane. Agate. Chalcedony. Chrysoprase. Cacholong. Heliotrope. Onyx. Sard. Sardonyx. Sardoine. Sardagate. Jasper.

Zircon. Garnets. Peridot. Olivine. Jade. Tourmaline. Lapis-lazuli. Malachite. Hematite.

> "Some seek amidst the pebbles of the stream
> The verdant beryl, or the diamond's gleam,
> Or where the bright green jasper meets their view,
> Or the clear topaz shows its lighter hue,
> Or the sweet amethyst which, serenely bright,
> Diffuses far and wide its tranquil light."

The stones of which we are now about to speak fall naturally into two classes, the first composed almost exclusively of silica, the second having a composition more complex. The latter class contain a considerable proportion of silica also, but it is always combined with one or more substances, the nature of which varies in every stone.

FIRST CLASS.

The stones comprised in this class may be

arranged, from an artistic point of view, into three very distinct sections.

The first includes all the stones formed of pure silica *crystallized.*

The second comprehends all the stones formed of pure silica *not crystallized.*

The third includes the stones formed of silica, always nearly pure, but containing some traces of colouring substances, which, however insignificant their quantity, communicate, in a commercial and artistic sense, a value to the stones that is altogether special.

In the first group are placed quartz or rock crystal, and all its varieties. The latter bear very different names in commerce, but their composition is almost identically the same. If a piece of white silk were cut into shreds, and each of these pieces plunged into a dye of different tint and intensity, a different name might easily be given to each fragment according to its colour; but its substance would still be the same. Quartz holds the same relation to the precious stones of the section we are about to consider, as the white silk would bear to the tinted morsels we have described.

FIRST SECTION.

QUARTZ.

Quartz, which is called also *rock crystal,* is one of

the substances most frequently occurring upon the surface of the earth, and probably also in its interior. "It forms," says an English writer, "about one-third of the mass of those immovable hills whose summits pierce the clouds, and nearly the whole of the mobile soil of the trackless desert rolling with the wind like the waves of the sea."

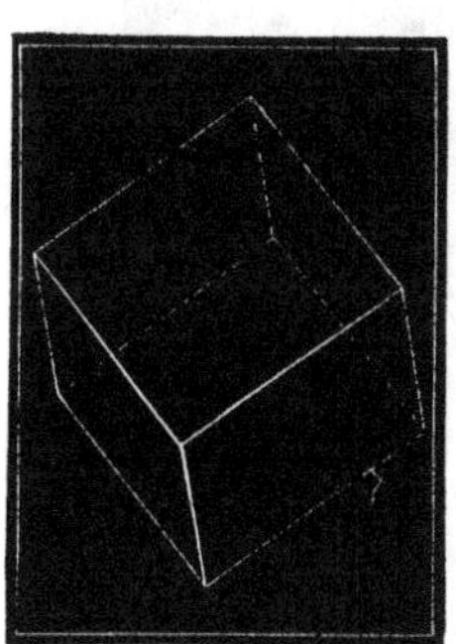

Fig. 67.—Primitive form of Quartz.

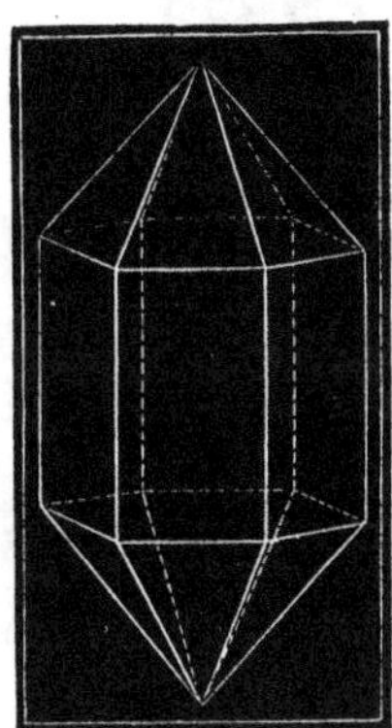

Fig. 68.—Most ordinary form of Quartz Crystals.

Crystals of quartz do not often occur of dimensions sufficiently great to attract the eyes of the common observer. Some magnificent specimens, however, are found in the ancient formations, which, as we have mentioned, are formed principally of silica: here indeed we would naturally look for them; but that which would seem much less probable, and yet actually occurs, is the presence of magnificent crystals of quartz, of an absolute purity, in the midst of rocks nearly exempt from all trace of silica; in Carrara marble, for example, and in certain gypseous formations in the south of France.

Quartz is formed by the union of two bodies; the one, *silicon*, is a substance analogous to carbon;

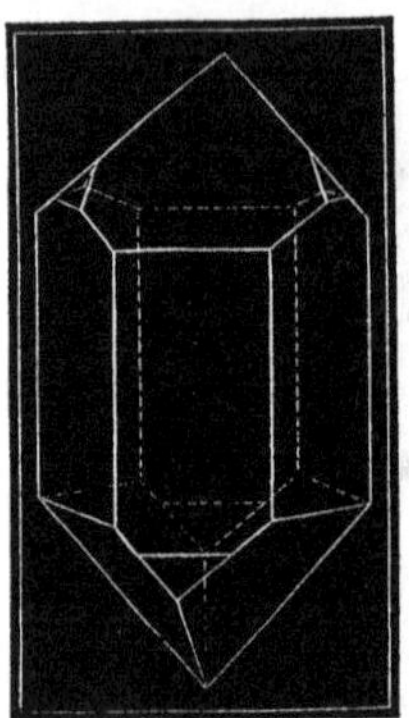
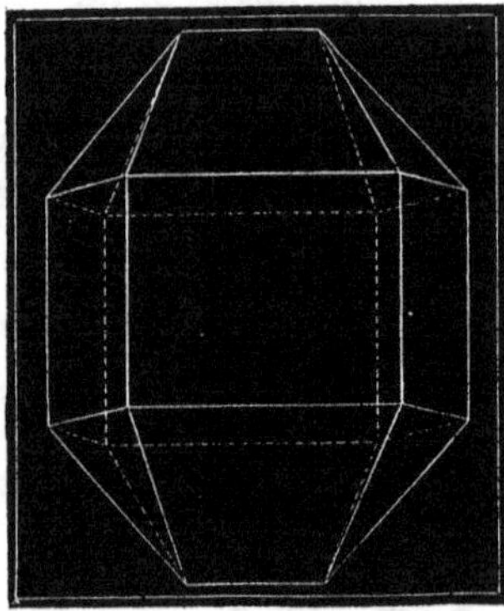

Figs. 69 and 70.—Modified Crystals of Quartz.

the other, *oxygen*, is a gas, and one of the principal constituents of atmospheric air.

The primitive form of quartz is the rhombohedron, but the primitive crystals are extremely rare. The most common form is the regular hexagonal prism terminated with six-sided pyramids (Fig. 68).

It is rare for the terminal pyramids to have all the faces equal. Ordinarily, on the contrary, three of these faces are developed at the expense of the other three, and thus we have the crystal represented by Fig. 69.

In other cases the crystals are not terminated by pyramids, but by ridges, as in Fig. 70. In this case the form of the crystals is greatly altered, and the regularity, to a certain extent, disappears.

If in the regular crystal (Fig. 68) we suppose the prismatic part to be diminished little by little without the form being otherwise changed, then, when

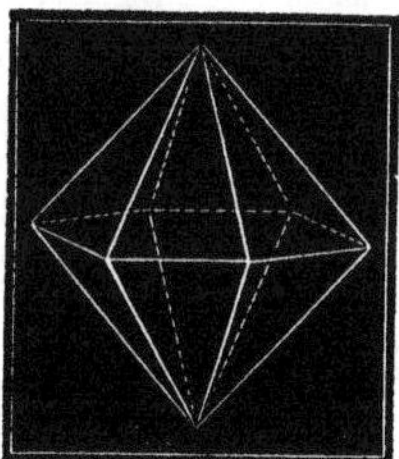

Fig. 71.—Dodecahedral Quartz.

the prismatic portion is quite removed, and the pyramids are applied base to base, the crystal represented by Fig. 71 is obtained. It is a dodecahedron, all of whose faces are equal, and bounded by isosceles triangles.

Crystals of this form occur in the midst of the gypsum which accompanies the *ophites* of the Pyrenees. Numerous examples of perfect purity occur also in the gypsum beds of Provence, which belong to the trias formation.

Crystals do not ordinarily attain large dimensions. For the greater number of minerals, crystals of 2 inches are almost gigantic: few indeed exceed 4 inches in height. Quartz, however, forms an exception to this rule. Specimens are brought from Madagascar more than 12 inches in length, and remarkably pure and transparent, notwithstanding their great size. The rock crystal of this island is used for the object-glasses of astronomical telescopes. Magnificent crystals have also been found in the Alps; one of these Alpine crystals, taken in Italy by the French, was borne in triumph to Paris in 1797. There is a beautiful specimen in the Museum of Natural History at Paris which measures 3 feet every way, and weighs nearly 800 pounds. It was found at Fischbach in the Valais.

At the French Exhibition of 1866, in the sections of Japan and of Brazil, there were some wonderful crystals. One crystal brought from Brazil weighs 212 pounds, is 2½ feet high, and 1 foot in diameter, and is a perfect six-sided prism.

A remarkable phenomenon in quartz is exhibited by the fluid drops which are contained in many specimens. Sir David Brewster ascertained that the fluid is not water, but of an oleaginous nature, one part volatile at twenty-seven degrees, and the other a fixed oil. Prof. Dana has named the former cryptoline, and the latter brewsterine.

Some beautiful specimens of quartz crystals, beaded with these imprisoned drops, have been found at Trenton Falls, in the state of New York.

EMPLOYMENT OF QUARTZ IN THE FINE ARTS.

Quartz has but little value of its own; but when it is made into vases, cups, and other artistic objects, it acquires a high price.

The Athenians produced some exquisite works of art in rock crystal, and the Romans valued it very highly in the form of vases. Nero had two cups of it, which he broke in his rage when he heard of the revolt that caused his downfall. One of these cups was estimated at over $1900.

The élégantes of Rome were in the habit of using balls of rock crystal to cool their hands, and certain occult charms were also said to reside in these cold smooth globes.

In the middle ages the Venetians produced some beautiful objects in rock crystal; and Milan has long been famous for its statuettes, vases, and girandoles of this material. But desire of gain has deteriorated the artistic value of these productions; cut crystals have come to be sold by *weight*, and the cutting is naturally falling into neglect.

In the cathedral at Milan the burial shrine of St. Charles Borromeo is wholly formed of plates of rock crystal of 6 or 8 inches square each, set in a framework of silver. The shrine was the gift of Philip IV. of Spain, who employed eight years in collecting the necessary quantity of rock crystal.

COLOURED QUARTZ.

When crystals of quartz are found combined with certain traces of colouring matter, they constitute distinct species in commerce, and take completely different names.

Combined with *iron* and *alumina* quartz becomes *yellow*, and takes the name of the *occidental* or *Bohemian topaz.*

Impregnated with a bituminous substance it becomes more or less darkened, and is called the *smoky topaz*, or *Alençon diamond.*

Combined with a slight proportion of oxide of manganese it takes a beautiful *violet* colour; it is then the *occidental amethyst.*

Coloured *blue* by iron and alumina, it becomes the *water sapphire.*

Coloured *rose* by iron and manganese, it is the *Bohemian* or *Brazilian ruby.*

Combined with a notable proportion of oxide of iron, it becomes a *brown red*, and constitutes the *hyacinth of Compostella.*

But among all these varieties there are only two

that are really valuable—the *amethyst* and the *water sapphire.*

OCCIDENTAL AMETHYST.

The amethyst, whose violet colour varies according to the quantity of oxide of manganese combined with the silica, has all the properties of quartz.

This substance is found in France, Prussia, Hungary, Arabia, Ceylon, Kamtschatka, &c. The environs of Carthagena in Spain furnish the most beautiful specimens of amethyst; and they are the more remarkable that they show a purple reflection vying with that of the oriental amethyst.

Brazil furnishes to commerce at the present day the greater number of amethysts. In that part of the world amethysts attain an enormous size. A block of amethyst, sent from the Brazils to Calcutta, is said to have weighed 98 pounds. Some of the Brazilian specimens are of two colours. The Count de Bournon possessed a cut and polished stone of this kind half violet and half yellow.

The ancients believed that wine, when drunk from an amethyst cup, lost the power of causing intoxication. Accordingly the attributes of Bacchus and Silenus are frequently found engraved upon ancient cups of amethyst.

WATER SAPPHIRE.

The water sapphire has nothing in common but the colour with the oriental sapphire; and even its colour—a clear white mixed with sky-blue—exhibits to the most inexperienced eyes a shade completely different from the magnificent velvety blue of the oriental sapphire.

There are water sapphires composed of nearly pure quartz; but those brought from *Ceylon* are of a much more complex composition. Somewhat more than half their weight is silica; the rest is a combination of alumina, magnesia, oxide of iron, and oxide of manganese. This variety is called *dichroite,* on account of its curious property of showing two very dissimilar colours when viewed from different sides—a *beautiful blue* in the direction of the axis, and a *yellow gray* in a direction perpendicular to this line.

IRIS.

Although this stone is no longer mounted by jewellers, and is only seen in antique jewels, it must not be passed over in silence; both because it was held at one time in high repute, and because it is liable to be confounded with several precious stones, particularly the opal.

The iris is a very limpid and very transparent

quartz. It is *crystallized*, a fact which immediately distinguishes it from the opal.

Under the influence of the light the iris is illumined with all the tints of the rainbow. This effect is produced by a great number of flaws and natural crevices contained in its interior; but its fires are always much less close than those of the opal.

Notwithstanding the neglect into which it has fallen, the iris was once very highly thought of. Much was said in the time of the First Empire of a certain parure of iris sometimes worn by the Empress Josephine. It is described among regal jewels in the Lapidarium of Marbodus:

> "By the Red Sea the swarthy Arabs glean
> The iris, splendent with the crystal's sheen;
> Its form six-sided, full of heaven's own light,
> Has justly gained the name of rainbow bright."

THE AVENTURINE.

The aventurine is a quartz of a clear brown or reddish-white colour, sprinkled with little spangles of yellow mica, that glitter like gold. It has been found also with a ground colour of yellow, of light gray, and of greenish-white.

The yellow variety has been called *sunstone.* It is very scarce, and exceedingly beautiful.

All aventurines do not owe their reflections and glitter to particles of mica. There is a kind—and that too pre-eminently esteemed—in which effects of this kind are produced by the presence of little crystals of quartz scattered through the mass, and reflecting the light on all sides. This last variety has generally a very clear tint of greenish-white, or sometimes of a reddish-brown.

The aventurine with mica was formerly brought from the borders of the White Sea; but at present it is furnished by Silesia, Bohemia, Siberia, and France. The species with crystals comes from Spain, and has for some years been produced by Scotland also.

Many substances are sold in commerce under the name of aventurine that produce similar effects, but are quite different in composition, particularly certain varieties of felspar, filled with flaws and minute fissures.

SECOND SECTION.

Before commencing the study of the stones comprised in this section, it is necessary to make an important remark.

So far the stones that we have examined are *crystallized*, and nearly always anhydrous. It is quite otherwise with those that are to be described in this group. They show no indication of crystallization, and nearly always contain water.

It is probable that their elements have never

been either melted by the direct action of heat, or deposited by the evaporation of a dissolving liquid. Everything, on the contrary, leads to the belief that they existed primitively in a gelatinous mass suspended in water.

Certain results produced by one of the grand

Fig. 72.—The Great Geyser (Opals and Chalcedonies).

natural phenomena of our own time sustain this opinion.

The boiling waters of the Iceland geysers—that at irregular intervals are projected upwards sometimes to the height of fifty yards into the air—are heavily charged with silica; and this substance, deposited little by little, produces at last enormous piles.

In these silicious masses are found branches of the birch-tree completely silicified, and in the midst of a reddish clay a thin layer of chalcedony, which, so long as it remains watery, is translucid, but when dry becomes opaque and like white enamel.

In these same deposits of the geysers small portions of silica are found, which perfectly resemble the noble opal so long as they remain hydrated; but they lose their vivid colours when they are dried.

M. Descloizeaux is disposed to conclude from this observation that opals and chalcedonies found in volcanic earths *had their origin in phenomena analogous to those of the Iceland geysers.*

THE OPAL.

The opal is formed of silica like the stones of the first group; but it differs from them by the constant presence in its composition of a certain quantity of water, making 5 to 12 parts in 100 of its weight. M. Damour has shown, moreover, that when sulphuric acid is applied to the opal the stone turns black, leading to the conclusion that it contains organic matter, probably bituminous. This the sulphuric acid would seem to destroy by setting its carbon at liberty.

The opal has no colour that may be called its own, but a faint bluish tinge analogous to the tint of certain resinous quartz, of which it is a variety.

Its true beauty and its great value are produced by a physical accident; it is traversed by a multitude of fissures filled with air and moisture, which reflect all the prismatic colours. The tender violet of the amethyst, the blue of the sapphire, the green of the emerald, the golden yellow of the topaz, and the flashing red of the ruby, appear at times isolated in certain parts of the stone, at times crossing each other in vivid play with an effect that is magical.

The opal is found in Arabia, Ceylon, Hungary, Saxony, Ireland, Iceland, Scotland, and Mexico.

Hungary and Mexico furnish the greater number to commerce; and some beautiful specimens have been recently brought from Honduras. The stones from all these places are true opals. Connoisseurs can usually distinguish the precise locality from which they are derived at a glance.

The opal occurs in veins or gangues in ancient formations, and is not scarce; but the parts that, after cutting, will display all the storied fire of the opal are very rare.

Beginning at the resinite quartz without fissures, and consequently without fire, and choosing successively fragments more and more closely fissured until the maximum is reached of the effect of light, an endless series of opals is obtained; but in commerce only three varieties are recognized—

The Oriental Opal.
The Fire Opal.
The Common Opal.

The *oriental opal,* called also the *noble opal* and the *harlequin opal,* shows generally in its fire a triangular disposition very characteristic. It exhibits flashes or flames of the most brilliant colours.

The affection that the ancients entertained for this beautiful gem was unbounded. The Roman senator Nonnius preferred exile to parting with a brilliant opal the size of a filbert, which Mark Antony coveted.

A very beautiful opal, considered by the virtuosi of Vienna and Dresden as the *third* in rank of the beautiful opals of the world, is described by Jack-

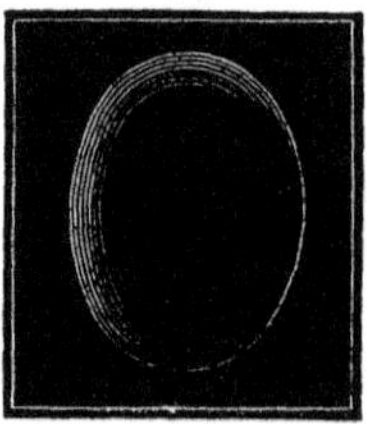

Fig. 73.—Opal of D'Augny.

son as having three longitudinal bands of the harlequin kind, from the uppermost of which rose perpendicularly the most resplendent flames. It measured nine lines by six. In the last century the two most famous opals belonged, one, round and very brilliant, to the amateur Fleury; the other, fascinatingly vivid—an oval of the dimensions of Fig. 73—to the distinguished financier D'Augny.

The *fire opal* is furnished principally by Mexico. Its colour, more pronounced than that of the oriental opal, and the carmine or vinous red tint of its fires, permits it to be easily recognized. At its maximum of effect the fire opal is brilliantly lovely; but its beauty is easily deteriorated by atmospheric influence.

The *common opal* displays very little fire; its colour is milk-white, which, joined to a texture extremely homogeneous, renders it semi-transparent.

It is said that since the opal was introduced by Sir Walter Scott into his novel of *Anne of Geierstein*, its favour has sensibly declined; and the gem, considered by the ancients to exercise the combined virtues of the amethyst, ruby, and emerald, is branded now as "an unlucky stone."

ENGRAVING UPON THE OPAL.

The work of engraving upon the opal is very difficult, and often quite impossible, on account of the thousand fissures of the stone. Besides, the fine effects of light which give it special value are only attainable in the maximum degree by simple polish.

An antique engraving upon a presumable opal is a head of Sappho; and in the collection of the Duke of Orleans was a head of Juba engraved upon an opal. There is, too, in the national collection at Paris, an opal engraved with a portrait of Louis XII.

THE HYDROPHANE.

The hydrophane, composed of 93 in 100 parts of silica, 2 of alumina, and 5 of water, is a very celebrated stone, known from early antiquity.

In its ordinary state the hydrophane is a white or reddish-yellow substance, feebly translucent or completely opaque. But if it is plunged into water it disengages little bubbles of gas, and at the same time becomes transparent, and sometimes displays the colours of the opal.

Taken from the water this curious stone keeps its transparency for a short time, but gradually as the water evaporates becomes once more opaque.

The ancient mineralogists, considering this stone an unexampled marvel, gave it the name of *Oculus Mundi*, the "eye of the world."

THIRD SECTION.

AGATE.

The agate, unlike other precious stones, very rarely occurs in veins; it is almost always in the state of concretions; sometimes in the form of geodes or balls. Occasionally there is found in the side of one of these balls a sort of funnel through which the silicious matter was introduced.

Sometimes the gelatinous silica has been abundant enough to give rise to homogeneous deposits of a certain depth; the stone in that case is of uniform colour; but often the deposits are in very thin layers, and of different shades of colour; often, too, they are moulded by the cavities of the body which forms their support, and take from its irregularities all sorts of dispositions with very variable shadings.

In cutting a section across a stone of this category, extremely different effects are obtained by following different directions. The varied zones and colours of the stone produce, too, infinite varieties; and descriptive names have been bestowed upon agates, according to these changes, as rainbow, cloud, moss, star, ruin, landscape, fortification agate, &c. The differences between all these varieties are extremely slight in a physical or chemical point of view.

Agates are divided naturally into two varieties:—

Agates of a single tint.
Agates of several tints.

FIRST VARIETY.

Chalcedony.—The chalcedony is quite a common stone, of a dull or milky-white; and sometimes of a bluish tint, when it is called *saphirine.*

The ancients obtained chalcedony from Egypt and Syria, and it was an object of considerable commerce at Carthage. It probably derived its modern designation from Karchēdōn, the Greek name for Carthage. It is found in England, Ireland, Germany, Italy, &c.

Chrysoprase.—Chalcedony coloured by the oxide of nickel, varying in colour from deep verdigris to the palest green. It takes a very beautiful polish, and fifty years ago was fashionable in jewelry, though now quite forgotten.

Cacholong.—A variety of chalcedony of a whitish tint, cloudy almost to opacity. It is found in Bokhara, Ireland, Greenland, and the Faroe Islands.

Cornelian.—A species of chalcedony, but of a finer grain. The ancients confounded it with the sardoine, and it was not until the thirteenth century, in the writings of Albertus Magnus, that the distinction became established.

The cornelian has sometimes the colour of polished horn; there is one variety that resembles the hyacinth, and another, of vermilion red, somewhat analogous to the ruby. Its colouring is due to the oxide of iron, and in certain varieties to organic matter, clearly discernible by analysis.

Heliotrope.—A translucid agate of a lively leek-green colour, spotted with red. The ancients used it, as Pliny tells us, for looking at eclipses of the sun, as we use smoked or stained glass; and it was said also to change the colours of the sun's rays into blood-red, when it was plunged into a vase of water. Hence the name *heliotrope*, from the Greek *helios*, the sun; and *trepo*, to turn.

SECOND VARIETY.

Onyx.—The onyx is the most celebrated variety of all the variously tinted agates.

Originally the name *onyx* was given to agates which had the appearance of a nail (Greek, *onyx*) where it joins the flesh; but it is now used for stones which exhibit marked contrasts of colour in bands, as black and white, or black and whitish-gray.

When an onyx unites in a desirable degree these conditions, it constitutes a stone of value, on account of the resources offered by it to the engraver, through the contrast of colours.

Sard.—This word, very anciently used, is said by Braunius to be derived from the Hebrew *sered*, "a red colour." However this may be, it is to agates of this colour that the name is applied.

Sardonyx.—A stone formed, as its name implies, of the sard and the onyx, using the latter term in its primitive signification. The sardonyx is a stone displaying alternate layers successively whitish and carnation red.

Sardoine.—Considered by many mineralogists as identical with sardonyx. Engravers, however, recognize between these two stones a marked difference: for them, the sardoine is an agate whose deep colour partakes both of yellow and red without either colour predominating. In colour, therefore, the sardoine differs completely from the sardonyx.

Sard-agate.—A semi-transparent stone formed of an inferior layer of orange-red or pale yellowish-red, and a superior layer of whitish tint, disposed one upon another with perfect regularity.

JASPER.

The precious jasper is the *jaspeh* of Aaron's breastplate; the *iaspis* of the Greeks.

"The property which distinguishes jasper from other varieties of quartz is its complete opacity even in thin flakes. Jasper is often a silex that has become opaque either by alteration that it has undergone, or by the addition of a certain quantity of oxide of iron, or of hydrate of the same oxide. There are red jaspers, brown jaspers, and green jaspers. In certain circumstances, as in the Egyptian pebble, the jasper presents irregular zones, which display a structure roughly concentric" (Dufrénoy).

It is one of the thousand varieties of rocks known under the name of *jaspers*. These varieties, hard enough to cut glass, present wide bands of diverse colours, generally red and green, upon a brown ground.

The silicious element predominates in the jaspers, but with it is associated certain bases (alumina, oxide of iron, &c.), sufficient to render the whole fusible under the flame of the ordinary blowpipe, which is not the case with quartz or its varieties that are very nearly pure.

The substances known in commerce under the name of jaspers differ so greatly from each other that their price varies from 20c. to $12 the pound.

ENGRAVING UPON AGATE, &c.

It is the agate, and the varieties of which it is the type, that have in all ages furnished to the engraver the stones best suited to his art.

One of the most remarkable engravings upon agate, and one of the finest specimens of this stone, is represented by Fig. 74. It is the bust of Alexander the Great. The head is carved in relief, and

Fig. 74.—Agate, Alexander the Great (reduced to three-quarters).

its colour is quite different from that of the groundwork of the stone. It is set in a superb frame of enamelled gold.

The fig. following (Fig. 75) is a chalcedony displaying a bacchic bull with an ivy wreath around his body and a thyrsus under his feet. It is one of the most celebrated of antique engraved gems, and bears the signature of the famous graver *Hyllus.*

As a specimen of modern engraving, we represent by Fig. 76 that celebrated stone known as the "seal of Michael Angelo." It is a small transparent cornelian engraved *en creux* or *entaille.* In the small

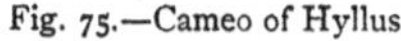

Fig. 75.—Cameo of Hyllus.

Fig. 76.—Seal of Michael Angelo.

space of an oval, hardly more than half an inch in length, there are fourteen figures, besides the scenery of a river with water-monsters and a fisherman. It is a bacchanalian or vintage scene, and it recalls a part of Michael Angelo's fresco of "Judith committing the head of Holophernes to her attendant." Critics are at variance concerning this cornelian: it has been ascribed to the famous engraver Pyrgotoles, with the supposition that Michael Angelo used its design as a passage of his great fresco; and, on the other hand, it is called a modern chef-d'œuvre, whose engraver has been inspired by Michael Angelo.

This stone was in the cabinet at Versailles, and was one day swallowed by an enthusiast in gems; but fortunately Hardion, who was exhibiting the treasures, observed the act, and before the honest man departed persuaded him to take an emetic for the benefit of his stomach. The gem was in this manner immediately recovered.

SECOND CLASS.

THE ZIRCON.

The zircon, called also the jargon, is altogether special in its composition, being formed of silica, united with a peculiar mineral—zircona, the oxide of zirconium.

The zircon crystallizes in four-sided prisms, with various modifications. Fig. 77 shows the primitive form, and Fig. 78 a modification approaching the form of the dodecahedron.

Generally speaking, each of the two types has its own particular colour, which is shared by the crystals belonging to it. The first is a brownish and greenish-yellow, the second brownish-red. Werner called the rhomboidal type *hyacinth*, and the prismatic *zircon.* Ancient lapidaries made the same distinction, and the stone that Werner calls zircon is their *jargon of Ceylon.*

The colourless crystals of the zircon are the most

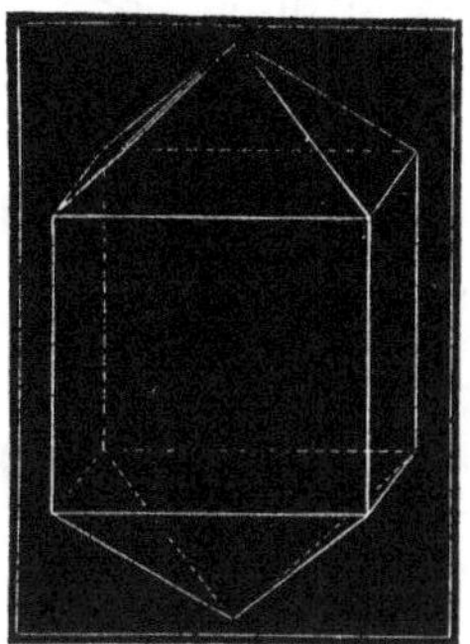

Fig. 77.—The Zircon.

Fig. 78.—Modified Zircon.

valued. They take on an excellent polish, display an adamantine lustre and fire, and will pass for diamonds if not too closely inspected. The zircon,

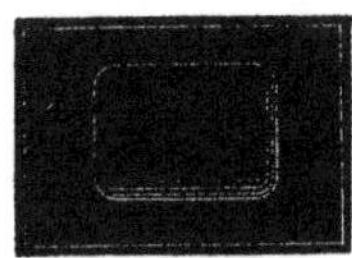

Fig. 79.—Zircon from the Cabinet of M. Drée.

accordingly, is sometimes introduced into ornaments, and sold to inexperienced people as a diamond, a particularly gross fraud, inasmuch as the zircon has but a very trifling value. Indeed even an exceptional zircon, of a beautiful olive-green tint, of the dimensions shown in Fig. 79, was sold at the auction of M. Drée for the sum of $16. A diamond of the same dimensions, even if only a rose, would weigh about 5 carats, and would bring not less than $1800.

The finest specimens of zircon are brought from Ceylon; but they are also found in Europe, in the vicinity of Lisbon, and in France, near the town of Puy.

GARNETS.

With materials which, though different in their nature, are cut and placed in the same manner, it is possible to construct several edifices resembling each other in form and disposition.

That which Art accomplishes more or less completely, Nature realizes perfectly.

Out of substances essentially differing in their nature she constructs well-defined and crystallized compounds, which appear to all intents and purposes identical, and yet are not so.

This phenomenon is called in science *isomorphism*, from the Greek *isos*, equal; and *morphē*, form. It was discovered by the celebrated German chemist Mitscherlich, and the discovery is considered one of the greatest scientific achievements of our century.

The group of minerals designated by the name of garnets furnishes one of the most remarkable applications of the grand theory of isomorphism.

Under this name are comprehended minerals differing much in colour, in specific gravity, in chemical composition, &c.; but whose fundamental form never changes, and which even presents a very

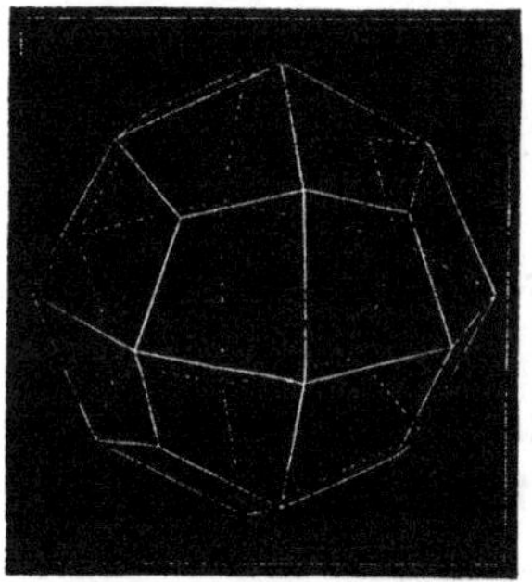

Fig. 80.—Garnet, Rhomboidal type. Fig. 81.—Garnet, Trapezohedral type.

small number of secondary modifications. Garnets are always crystallized, and they appertain to the tesseral system. Two secondary forms only are nearly always produced, the rhombic dodecahedron (Fig. 80), and the trapezohedron (Fig. 81).

In a scientific classification Rose, and the greater number of mineralogists with him, admit eight species of garnets, but two only furnish products for jewelry; these are:—

Grossularia.—This species is a double silicate of lime and alumina. As its constituents are colourless, either alone or combined, we should meet with limpid garnets devoid of any tint. Such garnets, in fact, are found in certain localities of Norway, Mexico, and the Ural Mountains. But as iron—which Haüy has called "the great colourist of nature"—is so extremely abundant, it becomes introduced in proportions more or less considerable into the grossularias, and the result is that the limpid garnets become tinted with green, clear red, orange red, &c., according to the quantity of iron combined. The varieties of Ala in Piedmont, so remarkable for the vivacity of their lustre and the purity of their forms, are grossularia. There are also certain yellow varieties in Siberia which resemble in colour the spinel ruby.

The analysis of a colourless garnet of the Ural has given the following results:—

Silica,	38·66
Alumina,	24·19
Lime,	37·15
	100·00

Almandine.—This species is a double silicate of alumina and iron; it is the grossularia with its lime replaced by oxide of iron. Often, however, the lime is not completely replaced, and the iron is not the only principle substituted, but then it is accompanied by an equivalent proportion of magnesia or oxide of manganese.

The beautiful variety of yellow garnet called *pyrope* belongs to the almandine species. It differs only from the type by a little quantity of the oxide of chromium taking the place of an equivalent quantity of the other bases. This substitution is regarded as perfectly regular by the mineralogist, but it produces a very agreeable colour, and gives commercially an altogether peculiar value to the *pyrope.*

It is to the almandine species also that the garnets so well known in commerce as *Bohemian garnets* belong. They are furnished by Bohemia, Saxony, and other parts of Germany.

The most desirable garnet is the oriental or Syrian garnet. Its composition varies, but its lustre and beauty place it above all others. Its name is not derived from Syria, as is often supposed, but from the Syrian, a river in the country called Pegu in Asia. It was from that country, indeed, that the first specimens were brought; but this commercial species is found equally in the Isle of Ceylon and in Brazil.

EXCEPTIONAL GARNETS, AND ARTISTIC APPLICATIONS OF THIS STONE.

At the sale of M. Drée's cabinet, a Syrian garnet of an octagonal form, $\frac{7}{10}$ inch by $\frac{6}{10}$, was sold for $650. Another, fire-red, 1 inch by $\frac{6}{10}$ inch, attained the price of $186.

Among engraved garnets may be mentioned the head of the dog Sirius, a chef-d'œuvre of Coli, a mask of Silenus crowned with vine-branches, a fine bust of Hadrian in the Odescalchi Museum, and a celebrated Venus Genetrix in the cabinet of the Abbé Pullini at Turin.

PERIDOTE, OLIVINE.

The peridote is a stone very anciently employed in jewelry; and as up till late years it was only found in water-worn fragments, its form of crystallization could not be determined. The recent discovery, however, of well-defined crystals of peridote on Vesuvius shows that they appertain to the right rhomboidal prism.

The peridote is a double silicate of magnesia and iron, with variable proportions of manganese, alumina, and sometimes nickel. According to the nature and quantity of the metallic compounds that enter into its composition, the peridote exhibits crystals of different colours. The peridote, properly so called, is a yellow-green; other varieties have clear olive-green tints, and are called by the lapidaries *olivines.*

The crystals of peridote are sometimes called *chrysolite,* but this must not be confounded with oriental chrysolite or cymophane.

An interesting fact attaches itself to the peridote. It is, among all the precious stones, the only one which has to this time had the honour of being found in those stones dropped from space, which we designate under the name of *aerolites.*

The peridotes of commerce are brought from the Levant by way of Constantinople, but the exact locality in which they are found is not known.

JADE.

This word is a generic term used to designate a certain number of substances, which, while resembling each other in many characteristics, differ materially in their composition.

These common characteristics are great hardness: wonderful tenacity, a wavy or scaly fracture, a certain oily lustre, and tints of white, greenish-white, milk-white, and rose-white.

The best known variety is brought from China; it is a silicate of lime and magnesia, with traces of oxide of iron, and sometimes of oxide of manganese.

Another variety, greatly prized by the ancients for its miraculous power of curing colics and the bites of venomous insects, is called nephritic jade, or nephrite stone; it is of a pale-green colour, sometimes with a slight tinge of lilac.

Antique objects made of jade are so hard that they can only be cut by the diamond; and as these objects are many of them of considerable dimensions, and their number is too great to suggest such difficult labour, it is supposed that when this jade was taken from the mine it was easily cut, and afterwards attained its hardness by exposure to the air, or perhaps by the direct action of fire.

The jade of Saussure, found in Switzerland, is a species differing somewhat from the Indian jade; and the *axe-stone* jade is a product of South America. It has been called the *amazon stone*, and Humboldt says that the Caribbees used the jade stone as amulets, cut in the shape of the Persepolitan cylinders, longitudinally perforated, and covered with inscriptions.

The principal mines of European jade are in Turkey and in Poland, where it is wrought into knife-handles, daggers, &c., and is softer than the oriental jade.

The Chinese are particularly fond of jade, and

work it into objects of great beauty. A sceptre of white jade was sent as a present from the Emperor of China to Prince Albert of England.

TOURMALINE.

The tourmaline holds but a secondary rank among those gems that are used for ornament, but, from a scientific point of view, it is well worth attention.

The modern tourmaline is the *lyncurium* of the ancients. It is also called *schorl*, especially in Germany, from the name of a village in Saxony, where it is very abundant.

Its composition is very complex; there are, however, certain elements which are characteristic of it, namely, boracic acid, silica, and alumina. In all tourmalines, also, there is an alkaline base, sometimes potash, sometimes soda, sometimes lithia, or a mixture of all. There is found in it also magnesia, lime, oxide of iron, and oxide of manganese.

The tourmaline is always crystallized, and its crystals appertain to the rhombohedral system. The crystals are in the form of longish prisms, sometimes with six faces, sometimes with nine, and in this case, in consequence of the obliteration or partial obliteration of faces, they terminate in such forms as shown in Fig. 82.

The tourmaline assumes a great many colours, and accordingly receives a great number of names. The Isle of Elba produces specimens from white to black; a species from Siberia is a beautiful red; from the Brazils both green and blue tourmalines are brought; and from Sweden a fine indigo-blue called indicolite. Berlin-blue tourmaline is called

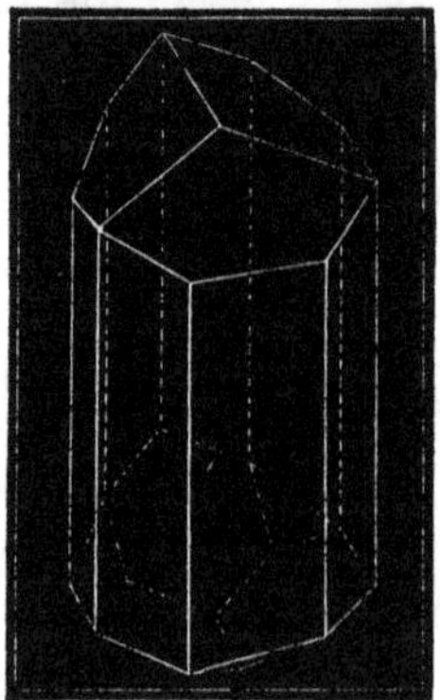

Fig. 82.—Tourmaline.

Brazilian sapphire; and there are green shades, which are called Ceylon or Brazilian emeralds.

These blue and green tourmalines show in the most pronounced manner the phenomenon of dichroism.

LABRADORITE.

The beautiful stone of Labrador, unknown until,

about a hundred years ago, it was discovered in the Island of St. Paul, near the coast of Labrador, is the type of one of the four great species formed by Rose, at the expense of the ancient group of the felspars. Its specific gravity is 2·6 to 2·7.

The labradorite is called sometimes the opaline felspar, because it resembles the opal in its beautiful reflections of colours. The finest colours are a play of blue and green upon gray. Yellow and bronze-red are less common; and a pearly-gray and purple-red still more rare.

The labradorite is essentially formed of silica, alumina, lime, and soda.

It has been found in its crystallized state scattered through volcanic productions, and notably in the lavas of Etna.

LAPIS-LAZULI.

The lapis-lazuli is a mineral whose beautiful blue colour varies from the palest tint to a deep blue, nearly black. The finest is a uniform colour of deep azure inclining to purple. Its specific gravity is 2·6.

Chemists differ in its analysis; but it is known to contain silica and alumina, with a supplement of soda, lime, and sulphur. Its colour is of such enduring quality that the preparation made from it, called *ultramarine*, is never deteriorated by the air, and is consequently of the utmost value to artists. Lapis-lazuli takes a beautiful polish, and is converted into many exquisite articles of ornament. It is found in Persia, Siberia, and Chili, but the most esteemed specimens are brought from China.

APPLICATION TO THE FINE ARTS OF LAPIS-LAZULI.

Lapis-lazuli is frequently engraved, and it is carved also into cups and vases.

The French crown jewels contained some beautiful objects in lapis-lazuli; among them a cup in the form of a boat, of large dimensions, and valued at $37,200, and a sabre with a handle of lapis-lazuli given to Louis XVI. by Tippoo-Saib, valued at $1116.

Many beautiful specimens were exhibited at the Paris Exhibition; exquisite carving by Rudolphi, a marine shell carved of azure lapis-lazuli, finely mounted by Morrel, and chef-d'œuvres by Duponchel and Jarny.

In the Orlof palace at St. Petersburg some of the apartments are lined with this beautiful stone.

MALACHITE.

Malachite, or "vert de montagne," is a hydrated carbonate of copper, or rather "a stalagmitic form of the green carbonate of copper" found in Siberia, Norway, and the Ural Mountains, and lately in South America. It is rarely found in masses weighing more than from ten to twenty pounds, and good specimens have a very high value. Its specific weight is 4.

Malachite takes a fine polish, and its varied shades of green, disposed with a thousand caprices, or in diverse zones, give it a pleasing effect. Beads and pendants of it are occasionally seen in jewelry, but its chief use in art is for ornaments of larger dimensions, such as boxes, paper-weights, statuettes, &c.

At St. Petersburg an exceptionally large slab of malachite 34 inches by 18 broad and 2 thick, is valued at $5294.

Under the First Empire an apartment in the Grand Trianon was furnished with beautiful objects all made of malachite, and presented to Napoleon I. by Alexander of Russia.

Attempts have been made to engrave malachite, but owing to its soft texture and multiplicity of zones destroying artistic effect, without successful results.

HEMATITE.

The hematite is a sesqui-oxide of iron occurring with a fibrous or radiated structure in mammillated or globular masses, and greatly resembles malachite in the mode of its formation.

It is a very common stone, of a dark-red colour, verging upon black. Properly speaking it is not a precious stone, but it is mentioned here because it is the first stone that ever was engraved. It is the material of the cylinders and the vases engraved by the Chaldeans, the Assyrians, the Medes and Persians, and Phenicians, in the remote time to which we refer the origin of art.

PART VI.

Pearl. Coral. Amber. Jet.

> " The sea-born shell conceals the unio round—
> Called by this name as always single found.
> One in one shell, for ne'er a larger race
> Within their pearly walls the valves embrace.
> At certain seasons do the oysters lie
> With valves wide gaping towards the teeming sky,
> And seize the falling dews, and pregnant breed
> The shining globules of th' ethereal seed."

The pearl is an animal product secreted by certain shell mollusca, of which one kind live in the sea, and the others in fresh water. Pearls are quite common, but those which have considerable dimensions, joined to a regular form and beautiful reflections, are rare and of high price.

Formed almost exclusively of lime and of an organic matter, the pearl is very easily acted on; as regards resistance, it has nothing in common with precious stones, even those most easily destroyed.

The pearl was dedicated to Venus. It is sacred to love and beauty. In the "marriage of Cupid and Psyche"—a fine engraving upon sardonyx, wherein the figures are enveloped in transparent veils, a work of great difficulty in engraving upon stone—the lovers are united by a string of pearls—emblem of conjugal bonds—by aid of which the god Hymen, bearing a torch, conducts them to the nuptial couch (Fig. 83).

Fig. 83.—Marriage of Cupid and Psyche, engraved upon a Sardonyx.

A number of opinions have been expressed upon the origin of the pearl. The ancients poetically ascribed it to a drop of dew falling at morning or evening into the opened shell.

> "Brighter the offspring of the morning dew,
> The evening yields a duskier birth to view."

It was once a common belief that the pearl was a morbid production of the animal. Above all, it has been thought that it originated in some foreign substance, such as a grain of sand, or an animal parasite, introduced accidentally into the shell. Thi. substance, it was supposed, tortured the animal, which, to free itself from the irritation, covered it with a pearly secretion. Acting on these ideas, the Chinese are said to have obtained pearls artificially, by piercing the shell, and slightly wounding the animal.

There is probably some truth in these hypotheses; but an examination of the pearl under the microscope proves that such modes of formation are not the only ones employed; and even that they do not necessarily enter into the formation of these beautiful productions. Indeed certain pearls show in their interior spherical cavities perfectly empty; and others, which are completely solid to the centre, display in all their parts a regular and continuous texture, without the least trace of any foreign matter.

A pearl of the first quality should possess, above all things, a fine *orient*, or water. By this expression is meant a pure whiteness, joined to a lively lustre that sparkles in the light. There are pearls, too, which, with a white colour, show *a delicate reflection of azure.* These are the most highly esteemed.

The second quality of a fine pearl is, that it should be perfectly spherical, or regularly pear-shaped.

There are a great number of pearls whose colour has a yellowish tinge. This alone is a mark of inferior quality.

It is very probable that pearls possessing this yellowish shade exist normally in the shell. Tavernier, however, thinks that all pearls are white, and that the yellow tint is induced by putrefied products, resulting from the treatment of the shells in their places of production; the pearl-shells being left in the open air that they may open of themselves after the death of the animal. The work is thus accomplished without any expense, and without risk of breaking the pearls, an accident that occurs very frequently if the shells are opened artificially. In support of his theory Tavernier states a fact, which, if established, would be conclusive; which is, that yellow pearls are never found in shells that have preserved their water.

The shells in which pearls are found belong to several families of the large class of mollusca; but the most important of all is the—

Avicula margaritifera, Bruguière; *Pentadina margaritifera,* Lamarck. This species not only produces the pearl, but furnishes to commerce vast quantities of mother-of-pearl of the kind most valued.

There is a prevailing idea that mother-of-pearl and the pearl are of the same nature; and, in consequence of this notion, numberless attempts have been made to obtain artificial pearls by means of little spheres more or less regularly cut out of mother-of-pearl.

The experiment has never been successful. A little serious examination of the subject proves that there is nothing to hope from this method. Even admitting that mother-of-pearl and pearl are the same in composition, which has not been scientifically proved, it is certain that they are not of the same constitution. Mother-of-pearl is much harder, and offers infinitely more resistance to the tools of the lapidary than the pearl. But that which is most important to be remarked is, that in the pearl the constituent layers are *concentric*, while in the pearls cut out of mother-of-pearl, the layers are more or less *parallel.*

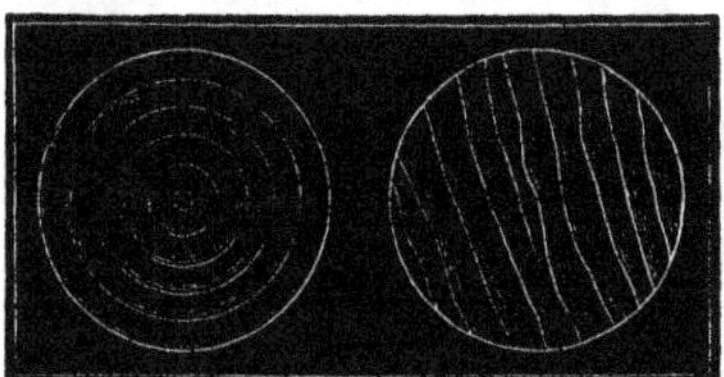

Fig. 84.—Pearl. Fig. 85.—Mother-of-pearl.

Figs. 84 and 85 establish perfectly to the eye the complete difference presented in this respect by mother-of-pearl and the pearl.

They show, at the same time, how the light must necessarily undergo very different modifications in the two cases, and why cut mother-of-pearl can never have the same optical effects as the pearl.

Although pearl molluscs exist in all parts of the world, there are but few places where their gathering has become an industry. One of these places was formerly the Red Sea, which, in the time of the Ptolemies, produced an abundance of pearls. But the beds are probably exhausted; at any rate they are no longer worked. The two regions which for a long time have produced the most beautiful pearls are the Persian Gulf, and the Straits of Manaar which separate Ceylon from the peninsula of India.

More recently great quantities of pearl-oysters have been discovered in America, particularly in the Gulf of Mexico, upon the coasts of California, and in the vicinity of Panama.

There have been experiments made to determine the time necessary to the development of a pearl. No very certain results have been obtained; but it has been proved that at least two or three years are necessary for the formation of a pearl of any value.

Hitherto the pearl shells have been gathered by divers, who, practising the pursuit from their earliest years, end by being able to stay nearly six minutes without breathing at the bottom of the sea. The prodigious efforts which they are obliged to make, and the considerable pressure to which they are subjected, result in a number of very grave accidents. The bodies, too, of the unhappy beings who devote themselves to this frightful trade, are very quickly covered with sores; and very seldom does a pearl-diver arrive at old age.

The remarkable appliances which render it possible to stay under the water for a long time without much inconvenience have been introduced into the localities where there are pearl fisheries, and will no doubt diminish wonderfully the sad consequences so long inseparable from this deadly trade.

Of all the objects employed as personal ornaments, the pearl is almost the only one that derives nothing from art. On the contrary, all attempts made to give it more value only end in deteriorating it.

Pearls were among the first substances ever employed as ornaments. As far back, indeed, as we can look into antiquity, we find them figuring in the first rank.

The Indian mythology speaks often of the pearl, and attributes its discovery to Vishnu, who searched the ocean for these ornaments to deck his daughter Pandaïa. The Book of Job and the Proverbs of Solomon also mention them. The accounts of ancient historians show the estimation in which pearls were held by the Babylonians, the Persians, and the Egyptians.

Everyone knows the famous story of Cleopatra, who, striving to rival the prodigality of Antony, dissolved in vinegar the pearl of one of her ear-rings, which had cost $706,800, and swallowed it. The possibility of this fact has been contested, but the thing is quite possible, only nothing more nauseous than the mixture can be imagined.

This experiment may possibly have been tried upon real pearls without success, but then probably the action of the acid did not last long enough. The pearl, as we have seen, is formed of carbonate of lime, and an organic substance. The vinegar easily effects a soluble combination with the carbonate of lime; but as soon as the lime of the first layer is consumed, the organic matter of a gelatinous consistence continues to envelop the pearl; and as this matter is not soluble in vinegar, nor can be attacked by it, a protection is formed around the interior layers, so that they are not reached by the corrosive liquid. But by persistence, in the end even this is penetrated, and the pearl is completely dissolved.

The passion of the Romans for pearls, like all the passions of this people, was carried to an extravagant height.

The pearl which Cæsar presented to Servilia,

sister of the celebrated Cato of Utica, had cost $223,200. The Empress Lollia Paulina, wife of Caligula, wore, in a set of ornaments composed of emeralds and pearls, the value of $1,488,000. Caligula himself, Nero, and other of those cruel men whom history is obliged to name among her Roman emperors, ornamented their buskins and strewed the furniture of their saloons with pearls. Under the influence of the ideas of which we have spoken in Part ii. pearls acquired great importance in medicine. Even in our own time they are frequently employed medicinally; and in China are chiefly valued on this account. Every year a large quantity are *absorbed*—generally in a dissolved state—by the inhabitants of the Celestial Empire.

By the effects of time, and of external agencies, pearls lose the beautiful reflections which constitute all their value; often, too, under these influences, they become more or less yellowish. There are also natural pearls, of a beautiful form and ample size, which do not exhibit these reflections, and whose colour is generally rather deep. In both cases they are called *dead pearls.* In this state they are of very little value, and a thousand means have been tried to give them lustre.

In certain cases the operation succeeds; in others it is a complete failure.

With great difficulty the present writer obtained

a certain number of *secret receipts* for restoring dead pearls to their primitive lustre. In one of these concoctions there are eighty-three ingredients, each one more whimsical than the last. In another the chief ingredient is dew gathered under certain conditions, and from the leaves of certain plants. One easily traces the influence here of the idea that the ancients entertained of the origin of the pearl.

At first glance these receipts seem only to associate the most dissimilar elements, and those that could not possibly have any efficacy; but the chemist discovers in them one remarkable fact: after the complex reactions of one substance upon another, there remains always the definite result of *an acid liquor*.

Recalling now the constitution of the pearl, formed of concentric layers, and the facility with which it is dissolved by an acid liquid, one can easily see that a pearl plunged into this liquor will be attacked, and that its exterior layer will quickly disappear. If the pearl submitted to this operation is only yellow and opaque exteriorly, the removal of the layer thus modified will leave bare the normal layers, and the pearl will recover its lustre. If, on the contrary, the layers are discoloured and opaque to the centre, nothing can restore it. In the first case the operation is a success; in the second it is a failure. The reason is no longer a mystery.

CELEBRATED PEARLS.

The most celebrated pearl which has been seen in modern times is described by the famous traveller Tavernier.

Found by an Arab in the neighbourhood of Catifa, it was purchased in 1633, by the King of Persia, for the sum of $260,400.

The pearl known as the *Peregrina*, bought by Philip II., king of Spain, weighed 134 carats; it was in the form of a pear, and of the size of a pigeon's egg. It came from Panama, and was estimated at more than 50,000 ducats.

Another still more famous pearl was brought from the Indies by Gorgibus of Calais, and presented to Philip IV., king of Spain; it had the form of a pear, and weighed 126 carats.

"How have you ventured," asked Philip IV. of the merchant, "to put all your fortune into such a little object?" "I knew that there was in the world the King of Spain to buy it of me," the merchant answered. There was but one royal way of rewarding such faith as this, and Philip IV. became forthwith the owner of the pearl of Gorgibus.

The inventory of 1789 shows that the crown of France possessed at that time pearls to the value of $186,000, among which occurred—

1st. A round virgin pearl of a magnificent orient, weighing about 27 carats, and estimated at $37,200.

2d. Two pear-shaped pearls, finely formed, and of a very beautiful orient, weighing both together $57\frac{11}{16}$ carats, and estimated at $55,800.

3d. Two other pairs of pearl pendants, weighing together $99\frac{6}{16}$ carats, estimated at $11,904.

There is also a magnificent pearl, which was brought from Berlin by the first Napoleon, and which was exquisitely mounted in a breastplate by Lemonnier.

When the Princess Royal of England was married to Prince Frederick William of Prussia she received, among other objects of jewelry, a magnificent necklace formed of thirty-two pearls. It is said that the pearls are not all of the first choice, but the necklace is valued at $93,000.

PRICE OF PEARLS.

Of all the substances employed in jewelry the pearl is the one whose value it is the most difficult to establish, because it depends upon so many variable conditions of size, form, and colour.

The table given here is one which was made by M. Harry Emanuel, to show the price of pearls of the first choice in 1867:—

		1865.	1867.
A Pearl of 3 grains,	. . . . .	$3·16 to $3·34	$3·90 to $4·27
" 4 "	. . . .	4·65 to 5·95	5·95 to 7·44
" 5 "	. . . .	7·62 to 9·67	8·55 to 10·78
" 6 "	. . . .	12·90 to 13·95	15·06 to 17·29
" 8 "	. . . .	19·34 to 23·80	21·57 to 35·85
" 10 "	. . . .	37·57 to 42·22	46·87 to 51·52
" 12 "	. . . .	56·17 to 70·30	65·47 to 74·95
" 14 "	. . . .	70·30 to 84·25	84·25 to 93·74
" 16 "	. . .	93·74 to 140·61	93·74 to 140·61
" 18 "	. . . .	140·61 to 186·93	140·61 to 186·93
" 20 "	. . . .	186·93 to 223·20	186·93 to 234·36
" 24 "	. . . .	281·23 to 337·59	281·23 to 337·59
" 30 "	. . . .	393·76 to 468·90	393·76 to 468·90

Besides the individual value which pearls possess in common with all other precious stones, and which is expressed in the preceding table, they have another very important one, which we may call *associative value.* Thus it happens, that two pearls of the same form, the same size, the same colour, &c., are worth a much higher price, if sold together, than when sold apart. A necklace, in which the pearls have been chosen from a great number, will be held at double the value of a necklace where the pearls have been picked from a smaller number, even when the individual value of the pearls is identical in both. In the first case the harmony will be complete; while in the second case the eye will detect a break in the shades in passing from one pearl to another.

CORAL.

Coral is a submarine production secreted by animals forming one little tribe in the grand class of polypi.

The colour of coral follows numberless gradations, from an intense red to a complete white. Its commercial value varies enormously according to its colour, the rose tints being the most esteemed. Different varieties are named according to the precise shade of colour, as "écume de sang," "rose," "fleur de sang," &c. One hundred shades of red coral are distinguished at Marseilles.

Until the eighteenth century it was believed that coral was a small tree living and developing itself under the sea. It was only in 1727 that a Frenchman, Peyssonnel, established its real nature, showing that the *flowers* of this *tree* were radiated animals, and that the coral was gradually formed by them.

Coral is fixed to the solid body which it rests upon by a kind of conical outspread foot. The nature of the support would seem to be a matter of indifference, so long as it is solid. The stems of coral are directed often in an opposite direction to those of plants, inasmuch as, being attached to the under side of rocks, they grow downwards.

The coral that is known in commerce presents itself in the form of little trees more or less branched; but in the living coral all the branches are covered with a sort of pale-coloured fleshy rind, glossy and polished, showing at its surface a great number of cells, each one of which incloses a polype. These very elegant little animals are what were taken for the flowers of coral.

Fig. 86 shows the polypi of the coral in different degrees of expansion.

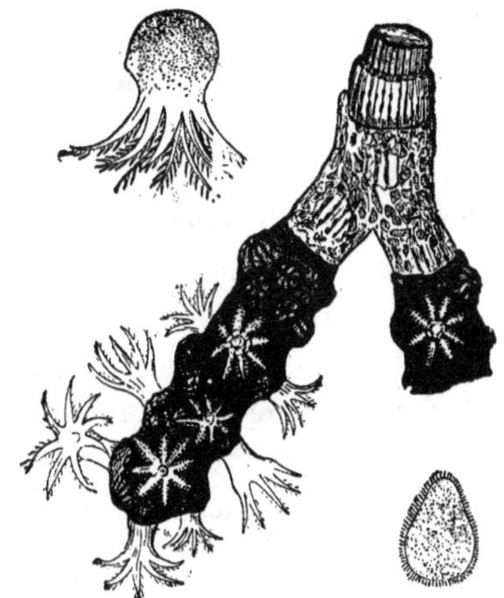

Fig. 86.—Polypes of Coral in different degrees of development.

It will be seen that their eight extended tentacules, pointed and incised along their edges, joined to the completely white colour of the animals themselves, present an *ensemble* which a century or two ago might well be taken for a flower.

Stripped of its coating, the coral shows a great number of parallel, longitudinal, and very often sinuous striæ, stretching from one end to the other of the axis. Its texture is extremely compact, this being precisely that which permits it to take a perfect polish, and gives it a great part of its value. But this texture is not homogeneous; on the contrary, it is perfectly organized. To be convinced of this we have but to break or cut a branch of coral perpendicularly to the axis, and to submit the part left bare to the action of an acid. The different parts will be unequally attacked, and a radiated texture becomes at once apparent.

Coral exists probably in all the seas of warm and temperate regions, but the Mediterranean furnishes to commerce the greater part of this product.

To gather it there has been for a long time used a sort of dredge called *salabre,* formed of two pieces of wood or iron, disposed in the form of a St. Andrew's cross, upon the extremities of which nets are fastened to receive the coral detached by the reiterated blows of the instrument.

There are also, as in the search for pearls, divers who plunge to a considerable depth to gather this beautiful production. But already the modern appliances for exploring the sea-depths have been employed with complete success to the gathering of coral.

There enters into the composition of coral 88 to 100 parts carbonate of lime, a little magnesia, some traces of organic matter, and about 1 part to the 100 of oxide of iron.

Coral possesses a very interesting property, which, beyond doubt, contributed to elevate it to the exceptional rank that it has occupied in medicine, even to the nineteenth century. Certain persons cannot wear against their skin any objects of coral without discolouring them, and this phenomenon is general among all invalids. The ancients asserted that if a person wearing a necklace of coral was on the verge of an illness, the coral showed discoloration before the least consciousness was felt of the approaching malady.

Naturalists and chemists have of course inquired what is the nature of this singular colouring matter that is so exceedingly impressionable? So far, the only colouring substance which chemistry has detected in coral is oxide of iron, one of the most fixed in nature, and one which, under the circumstances, cannot enter into new and colourless combinations; consequently the problem has not yet reached a solution.

AMBER.

Amber has been known from earliest antiquity. The celebrated founder of the Ionian school of philosophy, Thales, who lived 600 years before our era, speaks of the property which, above all, contributed to render it celebrated—that of attracting light bodies when it was rubbed. It is from the Greek name of amber, *electron*, that our modern term electricity is derived.

To explain the origin of amber, the Greeks had one of those graceful traditions characteristic of the young and marvellous genius of that people. They said that the sisters of Phaethon, weeping for the death of their brother, were changed into poplar trees upon the banks of the Eridanus (Po), and that their tears were transformed into amber.

It is to this legend that the tender and harmonious poet of the *Metamorphoses* alludes when he says:—

> "Stillataque sole rigescunt
> De ramis electra novis, quae lucidus amnis
> Excipit et nuribus mittit gestanda Latinis."

"The juices distilling from these new trees, solidified by the sun, are received by the shining river, and borne as offerings to the brides of Italy."

Chemical analysis shows that there are in 100 grammes of amber 81 grammes of carbon, 7·30 of hydrogen, 6·75 of oxygen, and some traces of clay, alumina, and silica, amounting altogether to about 3 grammes.

This is exactly the composition of resin; indeed amber is itself a resin.

"Amber," said Pliny, "trickles from the pith of

certain trees resembling pines." This quotation proves that the Roman naturalist considered amber as a contemporary production. He was right so far—amber is a resin; but it is a *fossil resin.*

The places most rich in amber are the borders of the Baltic Sea, between Dantzic and Memel; it is found also in Denmark, in Norway and Sweden, in Poland, France, and England, and in different parts of Asia and America.

Wherever amber is found it is associated with lignites. It is nearly certain that the resinous trees which produced these combustibles secreted amber, since it is not rare to find fragments of amber lodged in the midst of beds of lignite.

The presence of organized bodies, and particularly insects imprisoned in amber, was well known to the ancients, and is mentioned by the poet Martial in particular.

The illustration given here (Fig. 87) shows a lizard embedded in a piece of amber. The original fragment of amber belonged to the collection of Kircker, and was presented to him by the Duke of Brunswick.

The amber which is most esteemed is translucid, and of a beautiful lemon yellow; but there are also varieties semi-opaque, and one of a pale yellow with veins and spots of dead-white that is much esteemed.

Amber is worn as an ornament principally in the East, where it is cut into beads, and threaded as

Fig. 87.—Lizard imprisoned in a fragment of Amber.

necklaces. In western countries it is prized merely as serving to fabricate small objects of art, especially the mouth-pieces of pipes and cigars. This latter usage in the East is justified by the prevalent belief that amber never will allow the transmission of any infection. This of course would be a highly valuable quality, but unfortunately there is nothing to prove its existence.

Lumps of amber are generally very small, but occasionally a piece is obtained of considerable size; as, for example, a specimen of amber in the Royal Museum at Berlin, which weighs 18 pounds.

Amber is wrought on the turner's lathe by steel instruments, and polished on a leaden wheel with pumice-stone and water.

JET.

Jet, a beautiful black substance, is in point of fact a lignite produced by the decomposition of resinous vegetation buried in the earth thousands of ages before the historic times. Yet in mines of lignite jet is rare.

The hardness, the fineness, and the compactness of its tissue probably result from the peculiar nature of the trees from which it has arisen. However this may be, it is the union of these qualities that render jet capable of receiving a very brilliant polish, and assert its place as a valuable object of jewelry.

Jet is found in all places where amber exists,

and in many localities also where amber is not found.

Jet was formerly much more highly valued than at present. In the last century, Aude, in France, alone employed 1200 workmen on this substance. At Whitby, in Yorkshire, jet is still the object of a considerable industry. But the imitations of this substance have largely taken its place; even the poor imitation of varnished glass is received with favour. A much better substitute for it would be real stones of little value, such as black tourmaline, melanite, and obsidian.

Jet is worked by means of a lathe and horizontal sandstone wheels, smooth at the centre, but rough at their circumferences, so that the workman may cut and polish a stone on the same wheel.

Among ancient ornaments of jet are some curious anklets and bracelets belonging to the early period of British history.

A complete set of jet ornaments was found in two stone coffins deposited under the chief entrance of Saint Geréon, Cologne, when that church was repaired in 1846. They are supposed to have been the ornaments of some priestesses of Cybele.

PART VII.

Artificial Production of the Diamond. Boron Diamond—Cagniard de Latour—Gannal—MM. Despretz and de Chancourtois.

> "The liquid ore he drained
> Into fit moulds prepared, from which he formed
> First his own tools; then what might else be wrought."

Before we give an account of the attempts that have been made to produce the diamond by artificial means, it is necessary to state a few facts regarding two other simple bodies whose properties very closely resemble those of carbon, and which have an important bearing on the subject of which we are about to speak. These bodies are boron and silicon.

Not only do these bodies present exactly the three modifications presented by carbon—that is to say, they are either crystallized, graphitoid, or amorphous—but the crystallized boron so closely corresponds to the real diamond that it has been named from analogy the boron diamond.

Crystals of boron are limpid and transparent;

sometimes coloured garnet-red, and sometimes honey-yellow, by the presence of foreign matters. Their refrangibility can only be compared to that of the diamond, and they present the same effects of reflected and refracted light. They possess the quality of hardness, too, in such a degree as to scratch the oriental ruby and corundum; and M. Froment has used a crystal of boron to scratch the surface of a diamond.

The cutting of the diamond with powder of boron was attempted by M. Voorzanger, of Amsterdam, with entire success; only that a larger quantity was used than would have been necessary of diamond-dust, and the work was accomplished more slowly.

The same success attended the cutting of an exceedingly hard diamond in the collection of the Normal School at Paris. Its angular edges, and a furrow which marred it, were removed by a wheel covered with powder of boron. M. Guillot, who directed the experiment, confirmed the observation of M. Voorzanger concerning the superlative qualifications of boron-dust for cutting and polishing diamonds.

It has been further observed that the greater number of the powerful agents at the disposal of modern chemistry are without action upon boron. "It is," says M. Malaguti, "the most unalterable of simple bodies; and if the day comes when it can be obtained in large crystals, it may *replace the diamond.*"

Boron is extracted from boric acid, a production elaborated by nature in the depths of the earth, and whose appearance at the surface is one of the curiosities of natural chemistry.

In certain volcanic districts of Tuscany jets of hot steam, mixed with carbonic acid, nitrogen, hydrochloric acid, &c., and also a small quantity of boric acid, issue from openings in the soil called *soffioni* or *fumarolles.* Round these soffioni circular basins of various diameters are constructed, into which the water of neighbouring springs is conducted. The gaseous jets, forcing their way through the water, impregnate it with the boric acid, the quantity held in solution being increased by letting the water flow through a series of basins, in each of which it receives an additional supply of the acid. When it is sufficiently charged with the acid it is admitted into the final reservoir, where it is allowed to stand for a time and deposit its earthy particles. The clear solution is now run off, concentrated in boilers by the heat of the jets themselves, and the acid obtained by evaporation.

The manner in which MM. Deville and Voëhler obtained crystallized boron, once so difficult to obtain, is as follows:—

Into a charcoal crucible 80 grammes of aluminium is introduced in large morsels, and 100 grammes of boric acid reduced to fragments. This crucible is placed with charcoal paste in a crucible of plumbago, and the whole is subjected to the action of heat in a furnace producing a heat capable of easily melting pure nickel. This temperature is kept up for five hours; and when, after the cooling, the crucible is broken open, it is found to contain two distinct layers. The lower layer is vitreous, and formed of boric acid and alumina; the other is metallic, gray, and cavernulous, and is roughened and impregnated throughout its whole mass with little crystals: this is crystallized boron.

The mass in which these crystals are distributed is formed principally of aluminium, but it contains also variable quantities of iron and of silicon.

The whole is boiled in a lixivium of soda, of medium concentration, when the aluminium dissolves. That which remains is boiled with hydrochloric acid, and the iron is thus removed. The part not yet attacked is treated by a mixture of hydrofluoric acid and nitric acid, which removes the last traces of silicon. The boron, which has not experienced the slightest action under the influence of the preceding agents, remains as the definitive residue.

The boron thus obtained, however, is not perfectly pure; its analysis by M. Deville gives the following results:—

Boron,	89·1
Aluminium,	6·7
Carbon,	4·2
	100·00

It is very remarkable that this proportion of carbon (more than 4 to 100) does not prevent the boron from being transparent; and what is still more extraordinary is, that the boron becomes more and more transparent as the proportion of carbon increases.

M. Deville's conclusion is therefore inevitable, viz. that it is nearly certain that the carbon contained in the crystallized boron is present there in the state of *diamond.*

We perceive, then, that boron is worthy of the utmost attention, as being capable of affording a *special* diamond, and for its possible concurrence in the artificial production of real diamonds.

The properties of silicon being the same as those of boron, we need not pass them in review here.

ATTEMPTS TO PRODUCE THE DIAMOND.

Two hypotheses arrest consideration in examining the probable origin of the diamond; *the first* conceives of carbon as having been melted by a strong heat, and the diamond having crystallized in an excess of liquid; *the second* supposes a body capable of dissolving carbon, and allowing it to crystallize by evaporation.

Another theory was advanced by Sir David Brewster concerning the origin of the diamond. He supposed that this beautiful gem is of organic origin, and he was led to this opinion by examining the diamond microscopically, when he discovered certain striations and dispositions that resembled the fibres of organic substances, and particularly of certain species of wood.

These are but suppositions, however, and we really know nothing for certain regarding the origin of the diamond. The most we can say is that it is very improbable the diamond was produced under the action of a high temperature.

The knowledge of the chemical composition of the diamond is so recent that all the experiments made with the least chance of success to reproduce it have occurred within the last half century.

In 1828 two interesting experiments were made nearly at the same time by Cagniard de Latour and Gannal; De Latour presented his results to the Academy of Sciences, Oct. 10, 1828; and those of Gannal were presented the 23d of November the same year.

Cagniard de Latour sent to the Academy of Sciences ten tubes containing a number of light-brown crystals, some of which were of considerable dimensions. They were brilliant, transparent, and harder than quartz. They were examined by MM. Thenard and Dumas.

Submitted to an intense heat in contact with the air, the crystals experienced not the slightest change, a proof sufficient in itself that they were not of the nature of the diamond. Besides, notwithstanding their considerable hardness, they were easily scratched by the latter gem. The conclusion of the academical savants was, that the pretended diamonds were merely silicates or artificial precious stones.

The experiments of Gannal gained more renown. Specimens of his productions were sent to M. Champigny, director of the workrooms of the jeweller Petitot, who examined them with care; and having satisfied himself that they scratched steel, and could be scratched by no metal, that they were of pure water, and displayed a brilliant lustre, concluded that these little bodies were nothing else but diamonds. This declaration, emanating from a man well versed in the special trade, created an excitement and even a panic in the diamond trade.

The process by which Gannal obtained his diamonds was very simple.

He introduced carbon disulphide and water into a matrass, with morsels of phosphorus, which in the disulphide dissolved rapidly. He hoped that this phosphorus would slowly absorb the sulphur of the disulphide of carbon, and that the carbon, reduced gradually to an elementary state, would crystallize.

Carbon disulphide and water will not mix together; and the former being much the most dense, occupied the bottom of the vase.

Fig. 88.—Gannal's arrangement for the Production of the Diamond.

Between the two layers a pellicle formed which strongly reflected the light when exposed to it. In time this layer was augmented; and, at the end of several months it was composed of a conglomeration of little solid bodies, which were separated from the liquid by filtration through a chamois-skin. These little bodies were the crystals pronounced by M. Champigny to be diamonds—an opinion that was utterly erroneous. How they came there is not known, but it is probable that either the substances made use of were not pure, or that some foreign body or bodies had found their way into the matrass.

The man who has most effectually disturbed the slumbers of the possessors of diamonds, by agitating the question of their artificial reproduction, is M. Despretz.

This patient and persevering chemist organized a series of experiments founded at first on the belief that the diamond was formed by igneous means.

In his first attempts, accordingly, he submitted carbon to the action of the most intense heat that he could possibly command; having for this purpose united and arrayed all the Bunsen piles that he could procure at Paris, and so obtained a current of prodigious intensity.

The carbon was immediately reduced to vapour, and was soon deposited in the form of fine dust on the walls of the vessel in which it was contained. M. Despretz would have it that the carbon had been volatilized; and no one who attended his lectures at the Sorbonne can forget the profound disdain with which he would exhibit the glass globe all blackened interiorly, and exclaim, "And yet there are people who maintain that carbon cannot be volatilized!" With all due respect for this eminent opinion, it is probable that the carbon was *not* volatilized, using that word in its common acceptation, but that it was merely molecularly *dissociated.* However this may have been, the results were completely inadequate to the production of the diamond.

Violent means having failed, M. Despretz changed the system. For the currents of the pile, intense

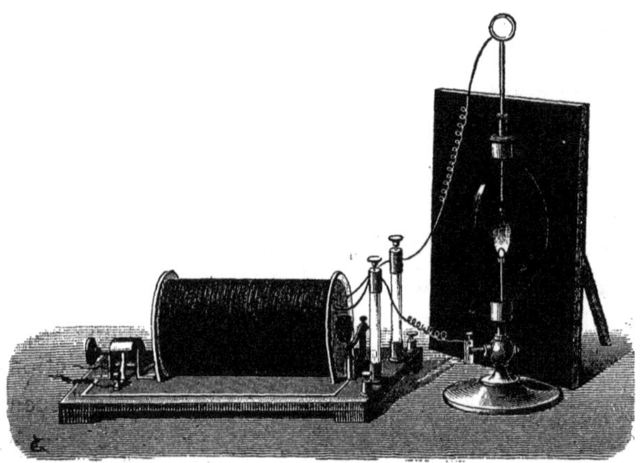

Fig. 89.—M. Despretz's arrangement for the Production of the Diamond.

and incessant, he substituted currents of induction, intermittent and feeble; and in place of continuing their action for several hours, maintained them in activity during entire months.

The results of his new experiments M. Despretz submitted to the Academy of Sciences.

He made use of a glass vessel similar and similarly fitted up to that known as the electric egg (see Fig. 89). To the lower rod he attached a cylinder of pure carbon, an inch or so in length, and nearly half an inch in diameter. To the upper rod he affixed a bundle of fine platina wires. He now exhausted the air from the balloon, and the distance from the wire to the carbon being about two inches, he then passed an inductive current by Ruhmkorff's apparatus.

The luminous arc was suffused with a red tint on the side next the carbon to a short distance from the platina; the part which enveloped the extremity of the platina wires was a violet-blue.

This disposition of the apparatus was constantly maintained; and the experiment lasted more than a month without interruption, excepting the time necessary to recharge the pile. At the completion of this time a slight black layer of carbon had been deposited on the wires. This layer, viewed through a magnifying glass, presented nothing very distinct; but to the compound microscope, with magnifying power of about thirty diameters, it offered several interesting features. Upon the wires, and especially upon their extremities, certain separate points were discoverable, which appeared to belong to octahedral crystals.

An experienced crystallographer confirmed this

view, and recognized octahedrons, both black and white, the black being truncated at their extremities.

In another experiment M. Despretz fixed a cylinder of pure carbon to the positive pole of a weak Daniell pile, and a platina wire to the other pole; he then plunged both poles into slightly acidulated water. The experiment lasted two months; the negative wire or pole became covered with a black coating, but nothing was discovered in it under the microscope.

The products of the experiments were then sent to M. Gaudin to test upon hard stones. He proved, in the presence of M. Despretz and others, that, mixed with a little oil, the substance which had enveloped one of the twelve platina wires sufficed to polish in a very little time several rubies. The black powder deposited in the water served to give similar polish, but it required longer time. As it is known that the diamond is the only substance that polishes the ruby, M. Gaudin did not hesitate to consider both these substances as the powder of the diamond.

Two conclusions may be derived from the facts we have just stated: 1st, that it is probable that the diamond is not of igneous origin; 2d, that M. Despretz has really obtained artificially the true diamond. This is the opinion of men of the highest authority, and in particular that of M. Dufrénoy.

The last contribution made to the interesting question of the production of the diamond was made by M. de Chancourtois. He based his theory upon phenomena presented by the solfataras, where sulphuretted hydrogen under the influence of a humid oxidization, is transformed slowly into water and sulphurous acid, and deposits crystallized sulphur. He proposed to produce upon carburetted hydrogen reactions of the same order. Under the influence of a humid oxidization all the hydrogen is transformed into water, *one part only* of the carbon into carbonic acid, and he thought it possible that the remainder, being slowly deposited, might crystallize and form diamonds. As a means of verification, M. de Chancourtois suggested the very slow passage of carburetted hydrogen in a mass of sand containing putrescible matter. Five years have elapsed since the expression of these views, and it does not appear that they have yet led to any positive result.

The question still remains—Is there any reasonable probability that the diamond will yet be produced artificially? This question we must answer in the affirmative. When it is considered how perfectly substances much more complex in composition, and complicated in crystalline constitution, have been artificially produced; when it is considered, too, what definite results were furnished by the second series of the experiments by M. Despretz—for in such a case the *size* of the crystals is a matter of indifference—there seems to be no reason for serious doubts of the possibility of the artificial reproduction of the diamond. Undoubtedly it will be a discovery from which the diamond-merchants and owners of diamonds will have much to suffer; but in this, as in other cases, the loss that will fall upon a small section of the community will be outweighed a thousand times by the advantages which arts and industry in general will derive from the discovery.

PART VIII.

Artificial Production of real Precious Stones. Results obtained. Becquerel. Ebelman. Gaudin. Henri Sainte-Claire Deville. De Sénarmont. Daubrée. Durocher. Sainte-Claire Deville and Caron, &c.

"Beset with emeralds
And diamonds, with sparkling rubies red
In checkerwise, by strange invention."

We have seen that the elementary constituents of precious stones must have existed once in a condition that allowed them to move freely; and that this condition was obtained by one of three general methods—

1st.—Direct fusion of the substance by a sufficient heat.

2d.—Dissolution at variable temperatures of the mineral substance in a foreign body, and complete or partial volatilization of the dissolvent; or crystallization without evaporation under the influence of natural forces, either alone or aided by heat, electricity, &c.

3d.—Prior reduction into vapour of substances destined to react upon each other.

To the *first method* belong the results of the observations of Mitscherlich upon the mineral species which are naturally produced in furnaces where metals are reduced; the direct reproduction of several minerals by Berthier; and, above all, the fusion of alumina and of silica, by M. Gaudin.

The *second method* comprehends the remarkable results of Ebelman; that which M. de Sénarmont has employed, but in which intervenes a new element, that of a very strong compression; and lastly, that of M. Becquerel, but with still another element, the action of a feeble electric current.

The *third method* includes the results obtained by MM. Daubrée, Ebelman, Durocher, Henri Sainte-Claire Deville and Caron, &c.

FIRST METHOD.

If any one should say—I am going to produce a fire of enormous power, without employing any substance but water, he would run the risk of being considered a fool, since fire and water have always been considered the antipodes of one another. Even modifying the announcement, and saying—I am about to produce an intense fire by means of elements derived exclusively from water, hardly makes the proposition appear more plausible, yet nothing can be more rigorously exact.

Water is composed of two bodies, which, in the present state of knowledge, are considered simple: they are two gases—one called oxygen, the other hydrogen. If a mixture of these two gases is made, and if to this mixture an ignited body is applied, the two gases combine and form water; but at the same time there is a production of vivid light, and a development of a great quantity of heat. These two effects attain their maximum when the mixture is formed of one volume of oxygen and two of hydrogen.

If, instead of forming the mixture immediately, we arrange so that the two gases arrive separately, in two uniform and continuous streams, at an orifice of small diameter, and if an ignited body is applied to this orifice where the gases meet and combine, the mixture takes fire. As the two gases are constantly renewed at the orifice, the combustion is not interrupted; and a jet of flame is attained analogous to that of a gas-burner. It gives out little light, but develops an exceedingly elevated temperature. The contrivance is called the oxyhydrogen blowpipe, and is in common use among chemists and others.

By aid of this instrument M. Gaudin melted silica and alumina, and artificially reproduced the corundum.

The corundum, as we have seen, is crystallized

alumina. To obtain it M. Gaudin heated ammonia alum and potash alum: the enormous heat developed by his apparatus volatilized the potash, and the alumina crystallized. Rubies were obtained in this manner; and M. Dufrénoy has found in these productions the rhombohedral form, and the triple cleavage proper to the corundum. Finally, M. Malaguti has established, by the analysis of these crystals, that they contain 97 to 100 parts of alumina, and 2 of silicate of lime; a composition analogous to that of the ruby.

The experiments of M. Gaudin date back to 1837; this date gives the priority to this ingenious physicist for the artificial production of the corundum.

It should nevertheless be noted that more than ten years before the work of M. Gaudin, a man who has left a deep impress on science, Berthier, basing his experiments upon chemical proportions, reproduced a great number of minerals, such as peridote, pyroxene, &c., by bringing their elements together at a high temperature.

SECOND METHOD.

In the year 1823 M. Becquerel, one of the most eminent of French physicists, formed the idea of using the currents of the voltaic pile to determine combinations, and not merely decompositions.

Instead of employing powerful currents, such as were used to produce decomposition, he applied to his purpose very feeble currents, and the results obtained surpassed his expectations.

The simple apparatus which he used is shown in Fig. 90. It is a tube curved in the form of the letter U. The curved part is filled with clay, to prevent the liquids contained in the branches from

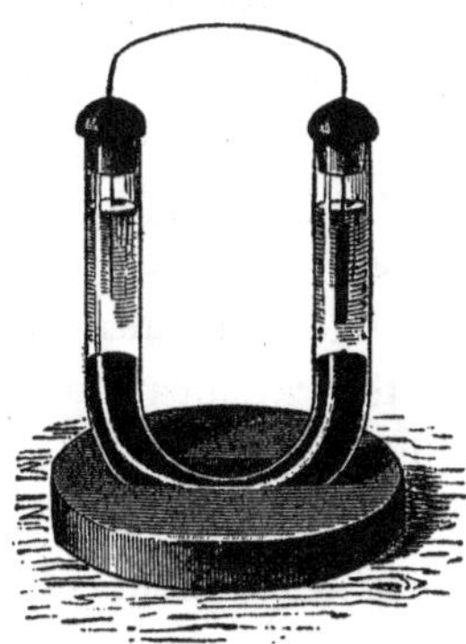

Fig. 90.—Voltaic Apparatus of M. Becquerel for the Production of Crystals.

flowing together, without interfering with the production of molecular actions and transports. The two liquids are, moreover, placed in direct communication by means of a metallic wire.

One of the substances reproduced by M. Becquerel was the sulphide of silver crystallized.

In the left branch of his tube he placed a saturated solution of nitrate of silver, in the right branch a solution of sulphide of potassium, and established a communication between the two liquids by the aid of a silver wire. Silver was deposited on the left-hand wire, and crystals of the double sulphide of silver and potassium on the right; but the sulphide of potassium being rapidly destroyed by the nitric acid, there remained on the wires in the clay, and on the walls of the tube, perfectly defined crystals of sulphide of silver, presenting all the characteristics of natural crystals. As the current was very weak, the crystals took long to form; some of them from seven to eight years.

The method by direct fusion could only be expected to produce fusible minerals. The electric method had given neither a silicate nor an aluminate; and, as crystallized bodies belonging to these classes are by far the most important, Ebelman set himself to solve the problem of their production.

Every one knows that if crystalline substances—such as salt, for instance—are dissolved in water, and the solution is allowed to stand in the open air, the water will disappear after a time, and the substance that was dissolved in it will be left in the shape of solid crystals.

Reasoning by analogy, then, Ebelman came to the conclusion that he must find some body capable of dissolving infusible combinations without contracting combinations with them, and capable of being reduced to vapour at a still higher temperature.

Experiment taught him that boric acid possessed the requisite properties in a high degree.

Being director of the manufactory of porcelain at Sèvres, he profited by the high temperatures developed in the furnaces to make some very interesting experiments, which were afterwards produced with still greater success at the continuous fires of furnaces placed at M. Ebelman's disposal by M. Bapterosses, fabricator of buttons of ceramic paste.

Mixtures in proportions corresponding to the composition of the stones to be produced were placed in capsules of platina along with boric acid, and the whole was submitted to a high temperature. The boric acid first melted, and afterwards volatilized, and, as Ebelman had anticipated, the substances that it held in solution crystallized.

In this way he produced the spinel ruby so perfectly that it could not be distinguished by Dufrénoy from the natural stone. This was effected by subjecting a compound consisting of proper proportions of alumina, magnesia, the green oxide of chromium and boric acid to a high temperature in the muffle of a furnace for eight days. He obtained crystals measuring 0·197 inch on a side.

The method employed by M. Sénarmont is *the method of dissolution by means of water.* It is, without doubt, the method employed by nature in caverns and calcareous crevasses, where, after a number of years, often very small stalactites of crystallized carbonate of lime are produced. These productions, and the phenomena of thermal springs, where the pressure and heat are often very high, and the deposits of mineral waters, suggested to M. de Sénarmont the method of his experiments.

He introduced into the most resisting sort of glass tubes the elements of the substances he wished to produce. He placed together gelatinous silica, and a body susceptible of furnishing carbonic acid by the action of heat (bicarbonate of soda), and having closed the tubes at the lamp, submitted them to variable temperatures and variable pressure.

By this process M. Sénarmont obtained a great number of crystallized minerals, the most remarkable of which was quartz.

THIRD METHOD.

M. Daubrée had pointed out in 1841 the principle upon which, in 1849, he produced artificially a certain number of crystallized minerals. The idea was to compel the vapour of water to react at a certain temperature upon the metallic fluorides, chlorides, &c., themselves brought to the state of vapour by the action of heat.

In these conditions a double decomposition is produced, and metallic oxides are formed, which crystallize.

Results of the same order are produced by introducing only the vapours of the metallic combinations destined to give rise to new bodies.

M. Daubrée obtained by this process a great number of species perfectly crystallized; among them the oxide of tin and quartz. Instead of making the vapours react upon each other, he made them react upon solids, and the results were no less satisfactory. It is by the employment of this method that M. Daubrée has produced first the apatite, and a compound having a close analogy to the topaz; and more lately has, by the use of the chlorides of silicon and aluminium, produced crystallized silicates and aluminates.

M. Durocher has obtained a great number of crystals by a method similar to that of M. Daubrée. The only essential differences between their processes is that Durocher used soluble combinations which pertained each one to the elements of the mineral he wished to crystallize, and Daubrée interposed vapours of water as a means of decomposing the generating vapours.

The latest experiments in the reproduction of crystals, and particularly of precious stones, have been made by MM. Deville and Caron. The method employed by these chemists is founded upon the same principle as those of Daubrée and Durocher; but the agencies employed by them are incomparably more powerful, and the results which they have obtained more brilliant.

With the enormous temperature developed by the furnaces of Deville and Caron ordinary crucibles could not be used: they melted like lead. The crucibles which they used were made of lime. Anybody can make them, and they are absolutely fireproof.

Among the principal results obtained by the experiments of these chemists were crystals of white corundum, rubies, and sapphires.

The crystals of corundum, nearly two-fifths of an inch in length, exhibited all the crystallographic and optical properties of the natural corundum. The rubies, obtained very nearly in the same way, had the violet-red tint of the natural ruby conveyed to them by the oxide of chromium, which furnished also, in a different proportion, the blue of the sapphires. Sometimes, in the experiments of Deville and Caron, red rubies and sapphires of the most beautiful blue were obtained side by side.

A similar experiment produced specimens of

cymophane identical in all respects with the cymophane found in America, in small but very perfectly formed crystals.

The processes we have just described are all distinguished by special features, though depending, as already mentioned, on a small number of laws. It is probable that nature has employed them by turns. In any case they suffice to explain the formation of the greater number of crystallized mineral substances at present known.

PART IX.

False Precious Stones.

> " Art, aping Nature, eager to deceive,
> Has learnt to imitate the jewel true
> With lying glass, and thus beguile the view.
> Hence hard the real gems from false to know,
> When pastes with imitative colours glow.
> Their boasted virtues soon as tested fail,
> And hence discredit does the true assail.
> Yet the true gem, by sages duly blest,
> In wondrous works its power will manifest."

Under the name of false precious stones, there are two kinds of productions which are essentially different—the one natural, the other artificial.

The first comprehends stones sufficiently hard to resist the file; they are generally quartz, either hyaline or variously coloured.

The second consists of artificial compositions of the nature of glass.

There is an intermediate order, the productions belonging to which, if well executed, are especially calculated to deceive, and are used to great extent in the East Indies. They are called semi-stones, or doublets.

FALSE PRECIOUS STONES OF THE NATURAL KIND.

It is of some importance to examine this subject, because there is a prevalent belief that all false stones necessarily have glass as their base, and are consequently of little hardness. People often say, when their rubies or their topazes are declared false, "But, see, here is a file; try to scratch these stones; you will not succeed." Very true; but submit any piece of quartz to the same test, and the result will be the same.

Since, as we have said, hyaline or variously coloured quartz is very abundant in nature, it is easy to procure, at insignificant prices, stones that perfectly resist the file, and show, often in a remarkable manner, the whole series of colours that we admire in real precious stones.

Stones of this kind are very abundant in commerce; it might be said that, with few exceptions, all those designated as occidental are of this character, and possess consequently hardly any value.

Another deception of the same kind consists in passing off a stone of a certain nature and a certain value, for another stone of a different nature and a much higher value.

The colourless varieties of sapphire and topaz, which in density, in hardness, and in refractive power differ but little from the diamond, are frequently cut into roses and brilliants, and sold for diamonds. A proof of this fact is furnished by the commercial price of the *colourless* topaz, which is much greater than it could obtain *as topaz*. It is valued in the secret hope that after cutting it may be sold for diamonds.

At the present day there are means—such as the scales for determining specific gravity, polariscopes, &c.—for distinguishing with mathematical certainty the diamond from the sapphire or topaz; but these tests are of modern origin; and in the middle ages not only colourless topazes, but those whose tint had been removed in different ways, principally by the action of fire, frequently passed current for diamonds. Nay more than this, under the influence of the ideas that then prevailed concerning transmutation, the successful experimenters believed that they had actually transformed rubies and topazes into diamonds.

Cardan furnishes some very curious details on this subject. He gives a receipt by which "a limpid sapphire of a faint colour" may be *boiled* in melted gold and converted into a true diamond.

SEMI-STONES OR DOUBLETS.

This mode of imitating real stones, though varying in a great many respects, is generally effected by giving the proper shape to a morsel of strass; removing from the upper portion of it a certain thickness, and replacing this by hard stone in such a way as to complete exactly the strass stone, then mounting the whole in a setting that completely conceals the line of junction of the two stones.

Doublets are of two kinds: in both the under part is strass, but in one the upper part is a plate of the real stone; in the other, it is simply hard stone, generally quartz, and of no value.

The invention of this process has been attributed to a modern jeweller of Paris, named Bourguignon; but in reality it can be traced as far back as the fifteenth century.

A complete description of the mode of manufacturing doublets is given by Cardan, who has even preserved for us the name of the inventor:—

"A fraud of a very bad character, and one very difficult to find out, was employed by Zocolino ——. This venerable personage used to take a thin flake of real precious stone, such as carbuncle, emerald, &c., when he wished to imitate the carbuncle or emerald, choosing such pieces as had but little colour, and were consequently very cheap. Underneath he placed a piece of crystal sufficiently thick, and united the two parts by means of a transparent glue, in which he incorporated a colouring matter in harmony with the stone that he meant to imitate—brilliant red for carbuncle, green for emerald, &c. He concealed the line of junction of the two parts by means of the setting; and to avoid giving rise to suspicion, he set them in gold, which was not allowed except in the case of real precious stones.

"In this way this magnificent workman deceived everybody, even the lapidaries. However, the fraud was at last discovered, and Zocolino took refuge in flight.

"It appears that this personage had a peculiar disposition for fraud, for he turned his attention afterwards to the fabrication of counterfeit money; and ended by being condemned to death."

An examination of the objects adorned with precious stones, that have been executed in the middle ages, shows that the process described by Cardan was not unfrequently employed.

FALSE PRECIOUS STONES OF THE ARTIFICIAL KIND.

The basis of all false stones of this kind is glass.

A fixed alkali (soda or potash) and silica heated to a red heat will combine and produce glass. Alumina, lime, magnesia, &c., may enter into the combination with the silica; but the result in both cases is colourless, or what is ordinarily called *white* glass. But if to these substances metallic oxides, or metals in a divided state, are added, even in minute quantities, the result is coloured glass.

Chemical analysis shows us that the elements of glass are found in all vegetables. If, then, a fire consumes a certain quantity of wood, gathered together at a single spot, vitrifications will be found in the residuum. When silicious stones are subjected to an intense heat, the bases contained in the stones and in the cinders combine and produce glass. This is what may be seen every day in an examination of the interior walls of a lime-kiln or brick-kiln. It is evident, then, that the discovery of glass belongs to the earliest period of man's existence. If it be remarked, besides, that the glass thus obtained is always coloured, and therefore in harmony with the pronounced taste of primitive people for brilliant objects, we understand how these vitreous substances produced by conflagrations and, above all, by the action of fire upon silicious stones, must have excited, in the most lively manner, the attention of men from the first ages of our species.

Had this book been written a dozen or fifteen years ago, it could have furnished but little information on this head; but, thanks to the researches of archæologists, and in particular those of M. Boucher de Perthes—for whom, no doubt, history reserves an exceptional place in its annals—humanity beholds its origin almost instantaneously extended far beyond the historic ages, far beyond all traditions! A new period, during which man lived upon our globe, and which has not until our own epoch been suspected, is now revealed in the most incontestable manner; and among the remains of human industry referable to that remote epoch,

Fig. 91.—Egyptian Bracelet in Ceramic Paste, with coloured Ornamentation.

are found objects of coloured glass. It must be remarked that coloured glass is much more easily obtained than glass without colour, and that the latter has been produced with ease only in quite modern times.

Without departing from historic times, but only reverting to their most ancient ages, we find that the Egyptians understood very early the manufacture of glass, and especially the coloured glasses.

The design of an Egyptian vase of blue glass, ornamented with white and yellow, is given in Fig. 92. In quality of material, in form, in elegance of ornamentation and harmony of colouring, this vase is in no respect inferior to the best productions of the present day, and yet it must have issued from the hands of the Egyptian workman four thousand years ago. In Figs. 91, 93, 94, 95, and 96, the objects represented are of ceramic paste. From

Fig. 92.—Egyptian Vase of Blue Glass, with white and yellow Ornaments.

an artistic point of view, these objects are of no value, but the delicacy of their details is well worth notice, especially when we consider that they must have been moulded when the matter was in a soft state.

Fig. 93.—Egyptian Moulding in Ceramic Paste.

In the time of Pliny, the manufacture of false stones was far advanced as a branch of industry

Fig. 94.—Egyptian Ring, with a Bezel of Ceramic Paste.

among the Romans. There existed several treatises

upon the subject; and Pliny declared that it was a difficult task to distinguish between the false and the true. Not only in Rome were false stones in vogue, but, according to Pliny, the Indians counterfeited jewels with success, especially opals.

The processes that Pliny was so careful not to divulge, were not held sacred with the same scrupulousness by the alchemists of the twelfth and thirteenth centuries. Both Albertus Magnus and St. Thomas Aquinas refer openly to this subject;

Fig. 95.—Egyptian Ring of Gold, with inlaid work of Enamel.

and the latter in his treatise on the *Essence of Minerals*, states explicitly that there were "men who fabricated artificial jewels." Among the precious stones counterfeited, he instances the hyacinth, sapphire, emerald, ruby, and topaz.

At the commencement of the Renaissance the fabrication of false stones still continued; but it was not yet separated from much hesitation and experiment. Cardan proves this in his curious receipts.

A century later we perceive by the descriptions

of Kircher that the industry had greatly advanced. To the unburned "brick" of Cardan, in whose cavity his mixture for precious stones was heated, excellent crucibles had succeeded; special furnaces had replaced the brick-kiln; and in the time of Kircher, that is to say, about the middle of the seventeenth century, false stones were no longer manufactured according to methods differing for each stone, but according to a general formula much the same as that followed at the present day.

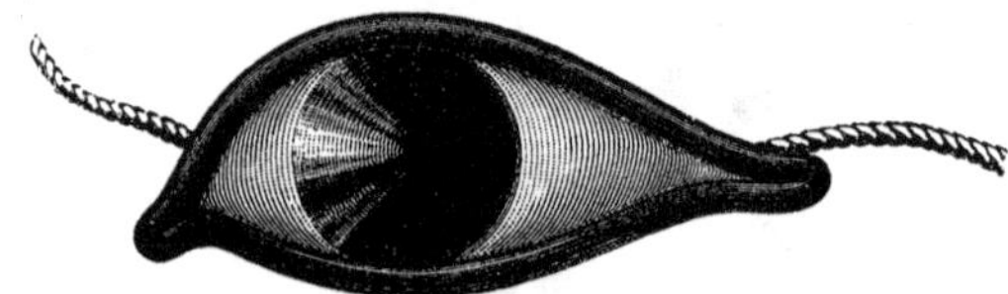

Fig. 96.—Egyptian Moulding in Ceramic Paste.

No other proof is needed than the writings of Kircher to dissipate the error that has ascribed the invention of *strass*—a peculiar kind of glass of considerable refractive power, which forms the base of all modern artificial gems—to a workman of that name, towards the close of the last century. This production was perfectly well known in the middle ages; and it was used for exactly the same purposes as it is used for to-day—for decoration, and the counterfeiting of precious stones. It is distinguished from ordinary glass by the presence of about 50 per cent. of oxide of lead among its constituents.

There existed in the middle ages, and probably had existed among the ancients also, a substance called at first *amasa*, then *encausta*, and lastly *smalta*, from which last term our modern *émail* (enamel) is derived. These were generic expressions for substances formed of glass and a metallic oxide; and the basis employed was certainly a kind of *strass*—that is to say, glass containing a great quantity of oxide of lead.

The improvement made in strass since the middle ages is due to our modern chemistry, which furnishes productions of a perfect purity, otherwise the ingredients, and probably their proportions, remain the same; and the same rule is still observed that the longer the fusion is prolonged, the finer will be the quality of the strass. According to M. Dumas, the strass now employed consists of—

Silica,	38·2
Red oxide of lead,	53·0
Calcined potash,	7·8
Calcined borax, alumina, and arsenious acid,	Traces.

When the strass is obtained very pure, all the precious stones may be imitated with it. For this purpose it is melted and mixed with substances having a metallic base, generally oxides, which, combining with the elements of the strass, communicate to it the most varied colours. We add a few details to show how the principal gems may be imitated.

Diamond.—The diamond being colourless, pure strass, cut into brilliants and roses, is used to counterfeit it.

Ruby.—1000 parts strass, 40 glass of antimony, 1 purple of Cassius, and 1, in excess, of gold.

Sapphire.—1000 parts strass, and 25 oxide of cobalt.

Topaz.—Same formula as that of the ruby, without the excess of gold, and heated for a less time.

Emerald.—1000 parts strass, 8 oxide of copper, and 0·2 oxide of chromium.

Amethyst.—1000 parts strass, 25 oxide of cobalt, and a little oxide of manganese.

Garnet.—1000 parts strass, and a variable quantity of purple of Cassius, according to the shade to be obtained.

Aventurine.—For several centuries Venice has had the monopoly of the fabrication of aventurine; and even now, it is a Venetian artist, Bibaglia, who furnishes to commerce the artificial aventurine that is most highly prized.

Aventurine is a glass the base of which is soda ash, lime, and magnesia, coloured yellow by oxide of iron, and holding in suspension a large number of small particles of oxide of copper. The distribution of these particles in a regular manner through the whole vitreous mass appears to be the chief difficulty in its manufacture.

The dexterity requisite to accomplish this must be very difficult to attain, for the profits realized from the manufacture of aventurine are remarkably large. According to its quality, the artificial gem sells for $5 to $15 the pound, while the raw materials that enter into the composition of a pound of it are certainly not worth a quarter-dollar.

French chemists—M. Hautefeuille in 1860, and M. Pelouze in 1865—have published processes by which productions have been obtained equal to that of Venice, and, in the latter case, perhaps superior.

The new aventurine of M. Pelouze has a beautiful lustre, and a hardness exceeding that of glass and ordinary aventurine. It is obtained by melting together 250 parts sand, 100 parts carbonate of soda, 50 parts carbonate of lime, and 40 parts bichromate of potassium. It will be seen that by this formula the spangles with a basis of copper are replaced by spangles with a basis of chrome.

FALSE PEARLS.

False pearls are little hollow spheres of glass covered internally with a coating imitating the orient of natural pearls. Their fabrication comprehends two series of operations—the production of the sphere, and the introduction of the coating.

The spheres are produced by the glass-blower, who by aid of an enameller's lamp solders the extremity of a tube having the proper diameter, and blows into the tube when the substance is of the right consistency. In this way very regular little spheres are obtained, that serve for the composition of the ordinary quality of false pearls.

In pearls of great beauty the tube employed is slightly opalescent, and the glass-blower, besides, gives to the little spheres, while they are yet malleable, certain slight perceptible inequalities of surface, by gently tapping them with a small iron bar. This gives them a yet greater resemblance to natural pearls, which are very seldom absolutely regular.

No mention is made in ancient writers of artificial pearls being made, and it is not till we come down to the beginning of the sixteenth century that we find Venice had then established a reputation for this branch of industry.

At first the glass balls were filled with various materials, generally with a base of mercury. But in the year 1680 a rosary-maker named Jacquin conceived the idea of using, in the place of this mercurial mixture, a harmless substance that produced an infinitely more perfect colour.

This substance, the essence of orient, is formed

from the scales of the bleak or ablette, a little white fish which abounds in the Seine, the Marne, and the Loiret.

The fishes are rubbed rather roughly in pure water, contained in a large basin; the whole is then strained through a linen cloth, and left for several days to settle, when the water is drawn off. The sediment forms the *essence of orient.* It requires from 17,000 to 18,000 fishes to obtain 500 grammes (a little over a pound) of this substance.

The scaly substance is liable to decompose quickly, and numerous chemical agents are employed by different manufacturers to preserve it. These means are kept a secret, but it is known that liquid ammonia, or the volatile alkali, is one of the substances most commonly used.

The process of colouring the pearl is commenced by lining the interior of the ball with a delicate layer of perfectly limpid and colourless parchment-glue; and before it is quite dry, the essence of orient is introduced by means of a slender blow-pipe. It is then allowed to dry; the pearl is filled with wax, and, if intended for a necklace, is pierced.

FALSE CORAL.

A number of objects are made at the present day of a composition intended to resemble coral, but this imitation is by no means a success. It is a paste formed of marble dust and isinglass. The colour is given by a mixture of vermilion and minium incorporated with the mass.

ARTIFICIAL COLOURING OF HARD STONES USED BY ENGRAVERS.

The hard stones preferred by engravers are those which offer different tints or strongly-contrasted colours. As these vari-coloured stones are much more costly than stones of the same nature of a single colour, chemistry has been applied to for an artificial colouring; and the result is, that the greater part of hard stones engraved at the present day are artificially coloured.

The stone to be coloured is steeped in oil, and notwithstanding its apparent impermeability, is easily penetrated by the liquid. After being soaked a certain time, it is taken out, and, however perfectly it may be dried, a certain quantity of the oil always remains in its pores. It is then placed in a capsule, covered with sulphuric acid, and heated to boiling point: this heat is maintained until the sulphuric acid is evolved, when the stone is withdrawn and washed, and is found to have become black.

If the stone is of a quite homogeneous texture,

the blackness will be uniform; but if, as often happens, its constitution is not very regular, the most porous parts absorb the greater quantity of oil, and varied effects of colouring are produced, which furnish to the artist the desirable opposition of tints.

This operation can be easily explained. The oil being composed of the three elements—carbon, hydrogen, and oxygen, it follows that if the hydrogen and oxygen are removed, carbon remains. It is precisely this removal that sulphuric acid effects. Penetrating in the track of the oil into the pores of the stone, it determines the union and elimination of the hydrogen and oxygen, and leaves carbon diffused throughout the stone in a state of excessive division. It is these minute particles of carbon that impart a definite colour to the stone.

So far as regards the colouring, this process furnishes excellent results; but when it is asked, Should the prepared stone be considered equal to those coloured by nature? we must answer in the negative, notwithstanding the opinion generally held.

No doubt, in ordinary conditions, the fixity of carbon is absolute, but in this case we must remember that it is in a state of the most extreme division; and seeing that the natural porosity of the stone is increased by the sulphuric acid, and that porosity is highly favourable to the combination of bodies, it seems to be not impossible that in course of time the carbon may undergo a slow combustion, and the colour of the stone be more or less destroyed.

It is impossible, too, that a substance so corrosive as sulphuric acid should not make some impression on the stone. Silica, it is true, is not attacked by this liquid, but it is altered in a remarkable manner; and then precious stones of the agate class are not formed exclusively of silica, but contain small quantities of different substances on which sulphuric acid has a very decided effect.

The stones artificially coloured, then, may be used with great success for works of secondary value; but they should never be employed by veritable artists, who work "not for a day, but for all time."

PART X.

Cutting. Setting. Engraving of Precious Stones.

> " There is a fire
> And motion of the soul, which will not dwell
> In its own narrow being."

As we have already shown in our first part, precious stones are sometimes amorphous and sometimes crystallized, but even in the latter case they are almost always masked or very imperfect; and as much of their beauty, especially that of the diamond, depends upon what is called *play of light*, it is one of the first concerns of art to remove this mask and these imperfections.

For every species of precious stone known to us there exists one form better suited than all others to show to advantage the effects of the light, which undergoes different modifications according to the peculiar molecular constitution of the stone on which it falls.

The artistic series ot operations by which this desirable form is attained is called the cutting of precious stones. That of the diamond is the most important.

DIAMOND-CUTTING.

The discovery of diamond-cutting has been very generally attributed to Louis de Berquem, a resident of Bruges, in the year 1465; but in fact the actual discoveries of Berquem amounted only to the construction of a polishing-wheel, to be used with diamond-dust, and a systematic arrangement of the facets.

Long before his time diamonds were cut in India and China; and the inventory of the jewels of Louis of Anjou, drawn up between 1360 and 1368, included a number of cut diamonds. Indeed, 150 years before the advent of Berquem diamond-cutters had existed in Paris, one of these especially, named Herman, had made notable progress in his art by the beginning of the fifteenth century.

The grand centre of diamond-cutting in Berquem's time was the town of Bruges; but pupils of his passed to Amsterdam, Antwerp, and Paris, where they established other workshops for diamond-cutting. Those at Paris did not at first succeed, but afterwards, under the patronage of Mazarin, diamond-cutting took an important position at Paris. After the death of Mazarin this industry declined, and the revocation of the Edict of Nantes gave it a blow which it never recovered. At the present day Amsterdam is the head-quarters of this industry, and Mr. Coster's establishment in this city is the largest diamond-cutting establishment in the world. The art is still carried on at Paris, however, and also in London, and in both cities very successfully.

Diamond-cutting has also been introduced into America, where it is carried on in the establishment of Mr. Morse at Boston, and more recently at New York, by the diamond company under the direction of Mr. Hermann.

Diamonds are sometimes met with in their natural state in the form of well-defined crystals. It was no doubt these that first attracted men's attention, and for a long time they were the only ones to which any regard was paid. They are known as "native points."

The primitive form of the crystallized diamond, *the cube* (Fig. 98), is extremely rare; it hardly occurs once among a thousand diamonds.

The regular octahedron (Fig. 99) is a little more frequent.

The dodecahedron, either regular (Fig. 100), or with curved edges (Fig. 101), is a frequent form; but the most common form of all is the octahedron, with a six-sided pyramid on each of its faces.

Fig. 97.—View of Coster's Establishment at Amsterdam.

As already mentioned, there is little doubt that the first diamonds to which value was attached were natural crystals, that is to say, octahedrons or

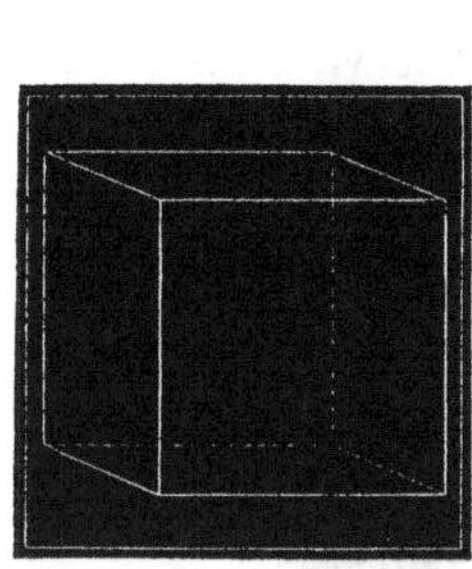

Fig. 98.—Cubic System.

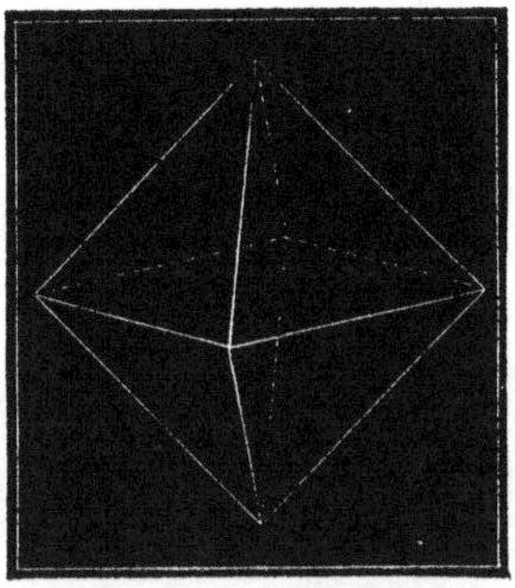

Fig. 99.—Regular Octahedron.

derived forms; and when the cutting of diamonds became known in the Indies, it was necessarily diamonds of this class that had to be operated upon.

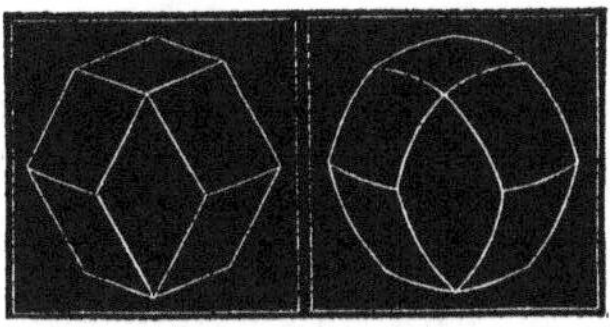

Figs. 100 and 101.—Common Forms of the Diamond.

Accordingly, when we examine the figures of ancient Indian diamonds given by Tavernier and Bernier, we find that the primitive style of cutting in India was to take an octahedron, replace one of the points by a plane perpendicular to the axis, treat the opposite point in the same way, but so as to have a plane much smaller than the first, and then cut four bezels round the principal face.

When the art of "splitting" became known, and it was possible by this process to obtain with ease flat-shaped diamonds of considerable size, the orientals took a fancy to stones of this kind, with their

Fig. 102.—Flat Diamond of the Grand Mogul.

four upper edges bevelled down exactly like the edges of ancient Venetian mirrors. Even at the present day this predilection has not disappeared, and similar stones are still those that are most highly prized by the inhabitants of India and Arabia. As an example of Indian cutting, we give a figure of a flat diamond that belonged to the Grand Mogul.

There are two principal forms into which diamonds are cut, the *brilliant* and the *rose*, both of them subordinate, in the first place, to the thickness of the stone. To each of these two types is attached a number of derivative and more simple forms.

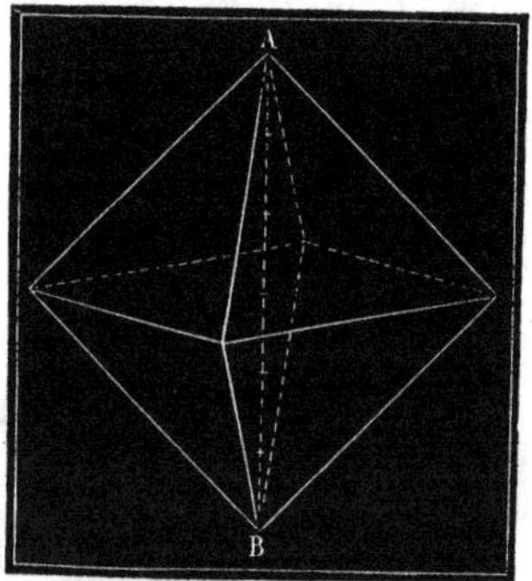

Fig. 103.—Natural Octahedral Diamond.

The starting point for the modern diamond, as for the ancient Indian form, is the simple octa-

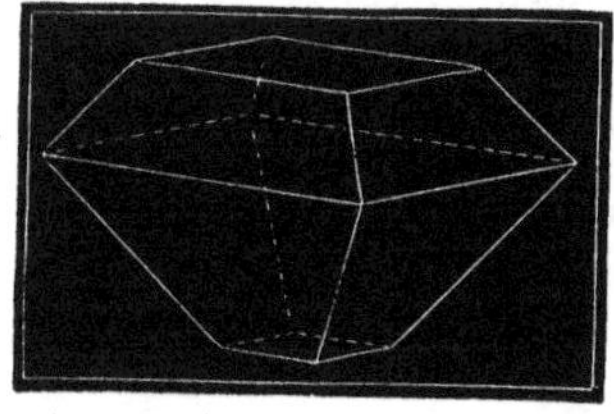

Fig. 104.

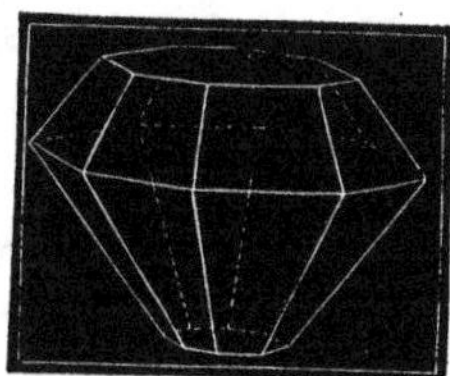

Fig. 105.

hedron. The following is the method employed in forming the octahedron into a brilliant:—

In Fig. 103 let the line AB which joins the two opposite summits, be divided into six equal parts, and let a plane perpendicular to the line AB pass through the second division from the upper point, and another plane also at right angles to AB pass through the first division from the lower point, then a small pyramid will be detached from each extremity, and there will remain the solid represented by Fig. 104.

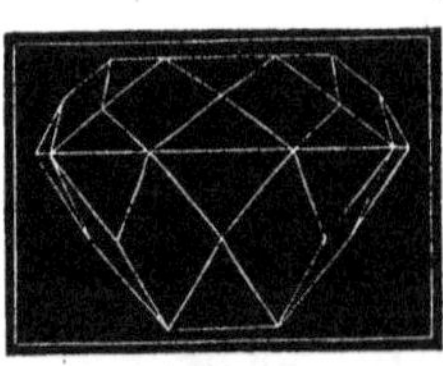

Fig. 106.

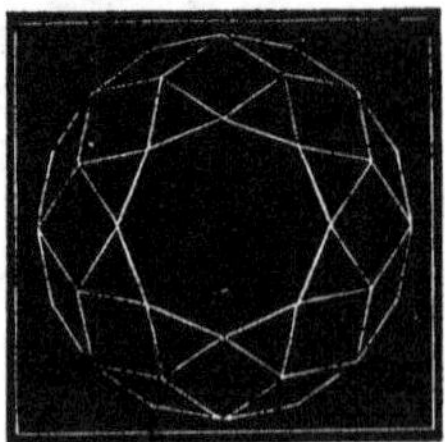

Fig. 107.

These are the proportions in which the axis is cut by the French lapidaries, but English lapidaries usually cut five-eighteenths from the upper pyramid, and one-eighteenth from the lower. The upper and larger plane surface is called *the table;* the lower is named *the collet* (French, *culasse*).

The four superior edges or *ribs*, and the four inferior edges, are then removed in such a way that the table and the collet are circumscribed by regular octagons, as represented by Fig. 105.

Lastly, the eight faces which limit the table are cut each into four facets, forming *the crown;* and the eight faces of the collet are divided in the same manner to obtain *the pavilion.*

The stone bears then sixty-four facets, besides the two parallel planes—the table and the collet. It is called the double-cut, or recut brilliant, and being the style which best displays all the beauties of the diamond, it is used at the present day for all stones of fine water and of sufficient depth. Figs. 106 and 107 represent this form as seen both vertically and horizontally.

Fig. 108.—Semi-brilliant.

The simple-cut brilliant has the same general form, but it has only eight facets above and eight below—sometimes only four—besides the table and collet.

There is another cutting for stones whose thickness is small in proportion to their surface. It is the semi-brilliant. It consists of the upper part of a double-cut brilliant, cut off at the line of junction between the crown and pavilion. This form is represented by Fig. 108.

THE ROSE.

In rose-cutting, the diamond is flat underneath; the upper and convex part is covered with a variable number of facets, systematically disposed around a first, of which the summit occupies the centre of the stone. If the stone bears twenty-four facets it is a "Holland Rose;" if it has but eighteen or twenty, it is a "Semi-Holland;" if the number of facets is diminished to twelve, or eight, or even six, it is an "Antwerp Rose."

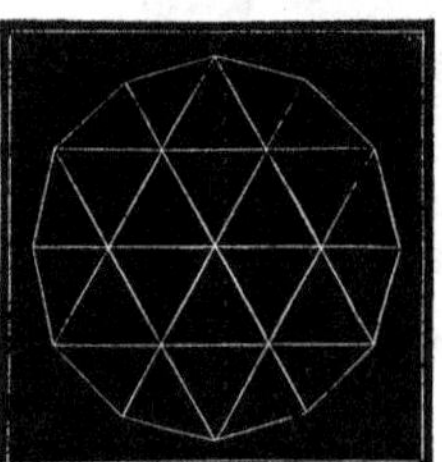

Fig. 109.—Holland Rose.

Sometimes rough diamonds, found in the form of pears, are covered with little facets, retaining the general form. These stones have the name of *briolettes;* they come exclusively from India, and are generally pierced in the upper part with a very small hole. No lapidary in Europe could drill such a hole in these diamonds.

There are also known in commerce stones cut

into *pendeloques* or pendants, in the form of a half-pear with table and collet, covered with facets on the collet side. They are very rare, and their price far exceeds that of brilliants of the same weight. Fig. 110 represents one of the pendeloques which Tavernier saw in India, and which its possessor would not part with for $11,160.

Another special form of cutting is that which was employed for "the Sancy." Diamonds cut in this

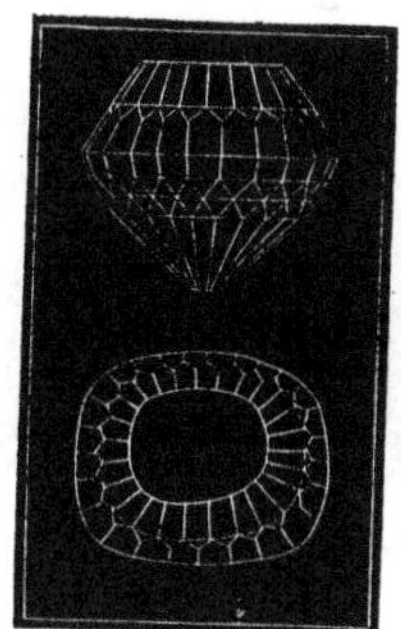

Fig. 110.—Pendeloque of Tavernier.

style have the form of flattened pears almost round, of a pendeloque shape, facetted both superiorly and inferiorly, and having a very small table above. M. Babinet thinks that this is the form in which both the Koh-i-noor and the Star of the South should have been cut.

There is also *the Star*, invented by Caire, and but little used. It was designed in order to take advantage of certain clear portions of rough diamonds, which could not be otherwise used without great sacrifice of material. Fig. 111 will show the appearance of stones cut in this manner. The form on the left represents the upper portion of the stone; the other two figures are alternative forms in which the lower portion of the stone may be cut.

The cutting of the diamond includes three series of operations: the *splitting* or *cleaving*; the *cutting*,

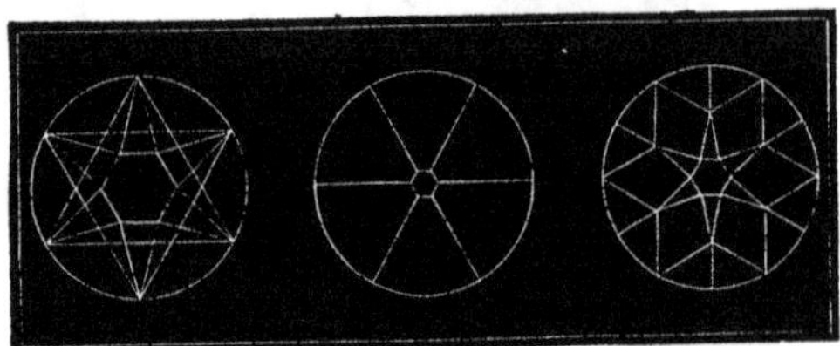

Fig. 111.—The Star invented by Caire.

properly so called; and the *polishing*. Special workmen are required for each one of these branches.[1]

It is to *the splitter* that the rough diamond is given; his quick penetration and ready action are to determine the future of the stone.

First of all, he examines very carefully the little

[1] The illustrations in this section relating to diamond-cutting are taken from fine water-colour drawings sent from Amsterdam and executed specially for this work.

morsel in his hand; he decides how it should be shaped to retain the utmost weight with the most brilliant effect; he detects every flaw and streak,

Fig. 113.—Details of a Compartment of the Splitter's Workroom.

and he knows whether the imperfections are at the stone's surface or at its heart. Very quickly then he sets to work. He takes a longish wooden implement or baton, shaped so as to be conveniently held in the hand, and having at one end a ferule extending a little beyond the wood and filled with a mastic or cement of resin and brick-dust. This cement he softens by heating it at a lamp, then

Fig. 114.—The Splitter.

embeds the diamond in it and lets the cement cool, by which means the diamond is firmly fixed in its place. With another diamond, sharply edged and secured in the same way, he cuts a notch in the diamond he is about to split. This notch is of a V shape, and must lie exactly in the direction of the cleavage-plane of the stone—a result which, though apparently so difficult, is easily attained by the practised eye and dexterous hand of the workman. A box beneath his work catches the dust, and a little sieve sifts at once the diamond-powder from the particles of resin dropped.

When the notch is cut deep enough the workman places the wooden baton upright in a hole in a block of lead before him; then introducing with one hand the blunt edge of a small steel ruler into the notch of the diamond, with the other he strikes the ruler a smart blow with a steel rod, and the stone is split. It is not without emotion that one sees this blow given, for the slightest error may prove fatal to the diamond's value for ever; but it is given without hesitation and with perfect composure.

The stone, which is now divided into two parts, is removed from the cement; the main part undergoes a repetition of the operation until it has received its proper form and all flaws are removed; and the fragments are carefully preserved to be cut into little roses, which, however small, have a value.

In Fig. 112 a general view is given of the room in which the splitters work in Coster's establishment at Amsterdam. Fig. 113 shows on a larger scale the complete arrangement of every division in this vast workroom.

Fig. 115 is an illustration of the diamond-splitter's

table. The reader will see on the left the blunt-edged steel rulers and the iron rod, somewhat in the shape of a double cone, which serves as a hammer; on the right, a saucer containing diamonds, and supporting a pair of pincers, and a lamp; in front, a handle having the sharp-edged cutting diamond

Fig. 115.—Table of the Splitter.

attached, and, standing upright, the wooden implement which supports the diamond intended to be split; in the background is a globe of water for concentrating the light at such points as more particularly require it.

From the splitter the diamond passes to *the cutter.*

At first sight the work appears to be exactly the same as at the table of the splitter. The cutter has two diamonds attached by cement to wooden handles, and the same sort of a box as the splitter has, to receive the diamond-dust. But the process

Fig. 116.—The Cutter.

is essentially different. Instead of cutting a notch in one of the diamonds, the cutter is slowly and laboriously grinding the two together in that mutual manner which accomplishes the smoothing of both stones. He is putting in practice the famous discovery which Louis de Berquem is falsely said to have made by chance, and, from the primitive form received from the splitter, he is shaping the facets of the brilliant or the rose.

The work requires great muscular force, and the hands of the cutters have to be supported by gloves—we might almost call them cases—of stiff leather. These gloves are seen in Fig. 117, which

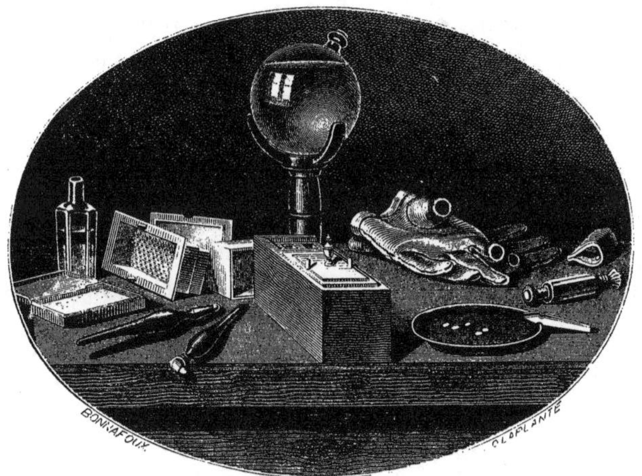

Fig. 117.—Diamond-cutter's Table.

represents the tools necessary to the work-table of the cutter.

A diamond, in the hands of the cutter, has not yet become an object of beauty; it has no lustre or transparency, and is even more unpromising in aspect than the rough diamond. The adamantine lustre, which is one of its special beauties; its transparency so pure; its refraction so powerful—all this is given to the diamond in the third phase of the cutting operation; and this phase belongs to the polisher.

The work of the cutter is not confined to the removal of the outer crust of the stones—he gives them the definite form which they are to preserve. If the stone is thick enough to produce a brilliant, he forms first the table, then the collet, and successively all the facets of the pavilion and the crown. It is easily seen that in all this labour a great deal of latitude is left to the cutter; but, as the final weight, and consequently the value of the stone, depends in a great measure on his skill, it is only tried workmen that are intrusted with valuable diamonds, such as those of larger size than four hundred to the carat. Smaller stones are made up in lots and delivered to the workmen after having been weighed.

So long as the diamond-cutter is engaged on a piece of work he shuts up the stones every evening in a little iron coffer provided with a padlock, of which he keeps the key. All these coffers, each with its number, are shut up after working hours in a large strong safe, and distributed to the workmen every morning. When the work is finished the large stones are weighed singly, the small stones in the lots, to see what the loss has been, and, according to the extent of this, the payment is greater or less. If a stone is found to be wanting in any of the lots, the workman has to pay a fine much greater than the value of the stone. As a

Fig. 118.—General View of the Polishing-room.

brilliant of five hundred to the carat, or still more, a rose of a thousand to the carat, are very small objects, it often happens that they are lost in the course of the manipulations they have to pass through. The floor, and the dust upon it, are then subjected to a most minute examination, in which a long silken broom is used.

The polishing comprehends two distinct operations—the *setting*, and the *polishing* properly so called.

The setter has at his command a furnace filled with burning charcoal. His work is to solder the diamond into a quantity of alloy resting in a brass or copper cup, which has attached to it a rod for holding it by. The alloy consists of a mixture of tin and lead, which, when pressed into the cup, gives to the whole the form of an acorn, with the diamond as its apex. This soldering is no easy task. There are sixty-four distinct surfaces to be smoothed in the brilliant, and each of these must be properly adjusted in the burning mould. It would seem that the fingers of the setters are fire-proof, for it is with their fingers that they adjust the setting of the metal around the diamond; and when, after its manipulation, the alloy is plunged into water to be cooled, the cloud of steam that arises attests the painful temperature to which the hand of the workman has been subjected.

The diamond, set as the apex of the acorn-shaped lump of metal, which again rests in a brazen cup with unyielding stem, is given to the polisher.

The polishing-rooms are the most interesting apartments of the great establishments for diamond-cutting, such as that of Mr. Coster at Amsterdam. Before revolving steel disks, that are running scrupulously parallel with the floor, and turning noiselessly with a speed of two thousand revolutions to the minute, are numerous workmen intent upon their task.

Fig. 119.—The Polisher.

The eyes of these polishers seem of little use compared with their sense of touch, which has been exquisitely educated. It is by the instinct of their finger-ends that the point of the diamond—kept constantly wet with mingled diamond-dust and olive-oil—is adjusted with determinate exactness of position, to the face of the revolving disk. It is clamped in a wooden rest, and the pressure is regulated by leaden weights, so that the diamond just touches the flying wheel. To the casual observer

Fig. 120.—Instruments used in Polishing.

the polishing art seems to be one requiring little skill or intelligence, but to acquire proficiency in the work requires years of assiduous toil.

From generation to generation the trade has been carried on, and the patient and monotonous toil and technical skill inherited and acquired by the finished workman is sure to be rewarded at last by a glittering surface from the hardest stone.

Sometimes months, and even years, are required for the perfecting of single stones. African diamonds are said to be particularly hard and difficult to polish; but, in the end, the most hopelessly resistant gem yields to the indefatigability of man.

In Fig. 120 are shown some of the objects connected with the polishing of diamonds. In the background towards the left the polishing wheel of steel is seen, and scattered over the table three of the copper cups, filled with alloy. The implement near the centre of the table, with the two upright pieces or feet at the left end of it, is for holding the diamond on the wheel during the operation of polishing. For this purpose it has a kind of vice at the end, in which the tail or stem of the copper cup is tightly screwed, and the whole then forms a sort of tripod, the cup which carries the diamond forming the third foot. The nut of the screw, and the key for turning it, are seen at the head of the implement. Its use will be understood from the cut showing the polisher at work (Fig. 119).

CUTTING OF PRECIOUS STONES OTHER THAN THE DIAMOND.

All the other precious stones are less hard than

the diamond, and they display besides the greatest difference from each other in this respect. Accordingly, though the processes followed in cutting them are not very dissimilar outwardly to those by which the diamond is cut and polished, yet the materials made use of are very different. The wheels have the same form and are set up in the same way, but they are made of much softer materials, and the powders with which they are covered are much less hard than diamond-dust.

Disks of lead, tin, or sometimes zinc, copper, and hard wood, are what the ordinary lapidaries use, and instead of diamond-dust they employ emery (a substance consisting chiefly of alumina), tripoli or rotten-stone (silica), tin-putty (bioxide of tin), and English red (anhydrous peroxide of iron). Different wheels and polishing substances are used according to the kind of stone. The greater part of colourless precious stones are cut with the leaden wheel, and with rotten-stone well moistened. This serves to give the first polish to all precious stones in which silica is the principal element—agates, jaspers, hyacinths, &c.

The two styles most employed are the *step-cut* and the smooth-cut or *cabochon.* When the latter is very flat it is called the "tallow-drop." Each of these may be round or oval, elongated or square.

The cabochon is plane, convex or concave on its

inferior side. In the latter case it is the double cabochon.

Concave cabochons are employed for stones moderately transparent, and this disposition tends to facilitate a more easy transmission of light. Garnets of a certain size are often cut in this form; and this cutting is used especially for the adularia, the cat's-eye, the hydrophane, and, above all, the opal.

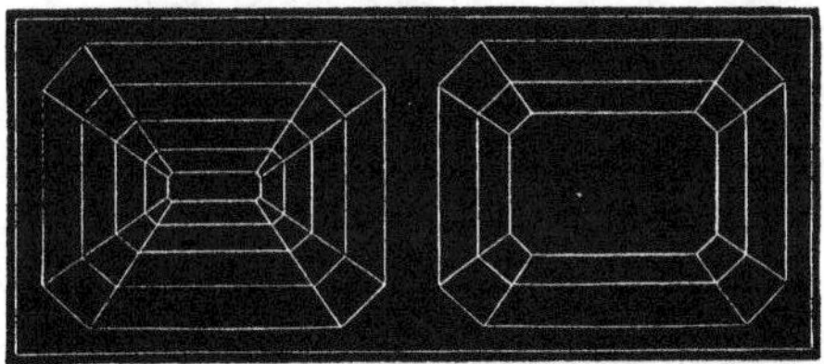

Fig. 121.—Cutting of Precious Stones other than the Diamond.

It serves better than any other form to display the special beauties of these different stones.

The stones cut in step or pavilion form are generally not very thick, and there are usually more steps or degrees on the lower than the upper side; as on the upper part a large table in the centre is generally reserved. Figs. 121 and 122 represent forms given to a great number of coloured stones, especially the emerald and the oriental aquamarine.

There are other forms, in which the stones cut in circles or ovals have a large table on the upper surface, surrounded with facets, which are either triangular or triangular and quadrangular both. In this case the lower face is covered with quadrilateral facets, and has a very small table in the centre.

Fig. 122.—Forms in which Stones are often cut.

Rubies and sapphires are frequently cut very much like the diamond, with this difference, that there is less thickness given to their upper part.

MOUNTING OF PRECIOUS STONES.

Precious stones, which enter into jewelry in a thousand ways, are rarely seen simply pierced and suspended as a drop; on the contrary, they are nearly always elaborately mounted in silver or gold. At the present day gold is used almost exclusively for the setting both of colourless and coloured stones; but silver is considered more artistic for the former, as it preserves their limpidity and brilliancy, and even lends them additional splendour, as gold does to the coloured stones.

There are two modes of mounting precious stones—one, which leaves only the upper part visible, called the close-setting; and the other, leaving the stone uncovered both above and below, called the open-setting.

A modification of the open-setting, called the knife-edge setting, leaving the edge of the stone clear, is used with beautiful effect for diamonds.

ENGRAVING OF PRECIOUS STONES.

When we examine the marvellous artistic productions, executed in cameo or intaglio, upon precious stones, we naturally think that the means employed must be numerous and complicated, but in reality the apparatus and the tools of the engraver are as simple as those of the lapidary. They consist of *the lathe*, and a series of little rods with heads of different shapes, all of which can be adjusted to the lathe.

The lathe, as will be seen from the appended figure, is a very simple affair. The axis, driven by the belt from the wheel, is pierced at the centre with an orifice, into which the tools for cutting the stone are firmly fixed by means of a screw. The engraver wets the extremity of the mounted rod with diamond-dust made into a paste with olive-oil, and as the wheel is in motion he applies the stone, properly prepared by the lapidary, and firmly cemented to a piece of reed, to the revolving tool. The diamond-dust enables the tool to cut into the

Fig. 123.—The Lathe at work.

stone with ease. As the design is frequently very elaborate and of the greatest delicacy, the tools are necessarily multiform.

Among the different varieties there are four most

used. The first is hollow; it describes circles with the utmost facility, and serves, when required, to perforate hard stones. The second is a disk quite blunt at the edge. The third is a sharp-edged disk of very frequent use, serving as a saw. The fourth is a rod, terminated by a little sphere, and is very frequently used. Fig. 124 shows all the tools used by the engraver.

As precious stones suitable for engraving have always a considerable and sometimes a very high value, it is important to be able to make use of every portion of them. They are therefore sawn instead of being ground down, so that the portion removed may also be made use of. This operation may be performed in different ways. The most ancient and simple method consists in fixing the stone to the extremity of a support, and cutting it by the friction of a bow, strung with two iron wires twisted together, and impregnated with diamond-dust. This method, however, is both tedious and irregular, and hence instruments, infinitely more rapid and precise, have been substituted for the bow.

Fig. 125 represents the mill of the lapidary, with the polishing disk replaced by a steel disk with a cutting edge, against which the workman applies the stone with his left hand, while he sets the apparatus in motion with his right. The disk is sprinkled with diamond-dust, which the workman collects

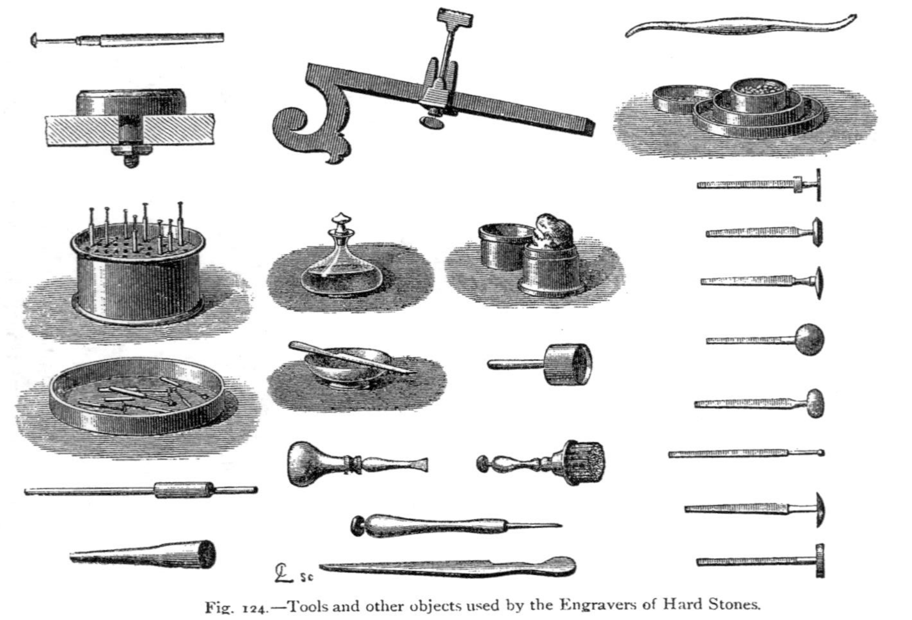

Fig. 124.—Tools and other objects used by the Engravers of Hard Stones.

and keeps always supplied to the edges of the wheel. This work is usually performed by the lapidary, preparatory to the engraver's task; indeed, the stone is sometimes set by the jeweller before it

Fig. 125.—Apparatus for Sawing Hard Stones.

is engraved, in which case it is embedded in cork. If it is merely shaped and not set, it is fastened upon a baton with lapidary's cement.

The tools and apparatus employed by the engraver are therefore very simple; but just as the sculptor, besides his chisel and block of marble, must have a certain amount of technical skill, and, above all, the artistic faculty, so is it with the engraver in hard stones.

To execute a high-class work of art on a stone of one colour is very difficult; but stones of different colours, and with the colours variously disposed, are those most commonly employed. Here the difficulty is enormously increased, for the artist, besides having to attend to the cutting, properly so called, has also to compose his design, and to observe that in working it out he takes the fullest advantage of the different colours of the stone.

We shall give one example to show the wonderful effects that are sometimes obtained by artists when working on stones of different colours. The design is that of a shepherd sitting on a rock with a staff in his hand. His face, hands, and legs are flesh colour; his coat has several holes in it through which his shirt appears; and the artist has taken advantage of a wood-coloured vein in the stone to represent his staff. Beside him is a tree with some green leaves on it, and having the trunk designed with the utmost fidelity.

Stones on which the design is raised above the general surface are called *cameos;* those having the design sunk below the surface are called *intaglios.*

The stones used for cameo-cutting are generally

opaque or semi-transparent, such as the onyx, sardonyx, cornelian, agate, &c. They are suited for subjects of the most varied character.

Intaglios are very often executed in transparent stones, and the subjects treated in this manner are more limited in number. They are chiefly such as seals, devices, coats of arms, &c.

In modern times Rome has almost a monopoly of this class of productions, exporting every year more than $50,000 worth of them.

In the Paris Exhibition of 1867 several magnificent cameos by Girometti were exhibited. One of these was a grand composition, representing Ptolemy Philadelphus and Arsinoe, valued at $6000, and executed on a superb oriental cornelian, which alone cost $2000.

Another design was an Achilles, on an oriental sardonyx, and valued at $2400. This was a striking example of the skilful manner in which artists may avail themselves of the different tints of a stone. The face of the hero seems bronzed by the sun, while his helmet and shield are of the colour of steel.

GENERAL CHARACTERISTICS OF PRECIOUS STONES.

Name.	Colour.	Composition.	System of Crystallization.	Specific Gravity.	Place in the Scale of Hardness.	Refraction.	Index of Refraction.	Dispersive Power.	Electrical Properties.	Fusibility.	Lustre.	Transparency.
Diamond, . .	White, yellow, blue, black, ...	Pure carbon.	Cubic.	3·4 to 3·6	10	Simple.	2·45 to 2·48	0·38	Positive.	Infusible.	Adamantine.	Very great.
Ruby, . . Sapphire, . Topaz, . . Emerald, Amethyst, (Oriental.)	Red, violet red, . . White, blue, violet, Yellow, ... Green, ... Violet, ...	Alumina, . . . 98·50 Iron and Lime, . 1·50	Rhomboidal.	3·9 to 4·2	9	Double.	1·76	0·026	Retentive of electricity for some hours.	Infusible.	Vitreous.	Complete.
Spinel Ruby, Balas Ruby,	Deep red, ... Violet rose, . . . Vinegar red, . . .	Alumina, . . . 69·00 Magnesia, . . . 26·00 Protox. of iron, . 0·75 Silica, ... 3·00 Oxide of chrome.	Cubic.	3·8	8	Simple.	1·75 to 1·80	0·04	None.	Infusible.	Vitreous.	Approaching completeness.
Chrysoberyl, Chrysolite, . Cymophane, . Cat's-Eye, .	Asparagus green, . Greenish, mixed with yellow, ... Greenish yellow, . Gray-green, with concentric veins,	Alumina, . . . 80·00 Glucina, . . . 20·00 Traces of oxide of iron, and oxide of copper. "		3 to 3·6	8·5	Double.	1·76	0·033	Retentive of electricity for several hours.	Infusible.	Vitreous and a little opalescent.	Transparent and semi-transparent.
Emerald, . Beryl, . . . Aquamarine,	Green, ... Bluish green, . . Sea-green, . . .	Silica, ... 68·00 Alumina, . . . 46·00 Glucina, . . . 12·00 Oxide of iron, . 1·00	Hexagonal Prism.	2·67 to 2·75	7·5 to 8	Double, but feeble.	1·58	0·026	Positive.	Not infusible.	Vitreous.	Feeble.

NAME.	COLOUR.	COMPOSITION.	System of Crystallization.	Specific Gravity.	Place in the Scale of Hardness.	Refraction.	Index of Refraction.	Dispersive Power.	Electrical Properties.	Fusibility	Lustre.	Transparency.
QUARTZ, . . . CHRYSOPRASE, OCCIDENTAL AMETHYST, JASPER, . . . AGATE, . . . CORNELIAN, . . ONYX, . . . SARDOINE, . . HELIOTROPE, .	White, smoky, . . Vert-de-gris, . . . Violet, ... Brown, green, red veins, ... Clear gray tints, . Red, often bright red, ... White, grayish, and dark brown, . . Fawn colour, . .	Silica. Traces of alumina, oxide of iron, &c.	Hexagonal Prism.	2·65	7	Double.	1·55	0·026	Positive.	In-fusible.	Vitreous.	Transparent.
OPAL, . . . HYDROPHANE,	Iridescent, . . . Gray white, often transparent when wet, ...	Silica, 91; water, 09·00 Silica, ... 93·00 Alumina, . . . 2·00 Water, . . . 5·00	Not Crystallized.	2·11 to 2·35	5·5 to 6·5	,,	,,	,,	,,	In-fusible.	Vitreous.	Feeble.
PERIDOTE, . . CHRYSOLITE, . OLIVINE, . .	Leek green, . . . Golden yellow, . . Greenish, ...	Silica, ... 30·75 Magnesia, . . . 50·04 Protoxide of iron, 9·19 ,, manganese, 0·09 ,, nickel, 0·32 Alumina, . . . 0·22	Oblique Rhomboidal Prism.	3·41 3·35 to 3·34	5·6	Double.	1·66	0·033	Acquiring electricity by friction.	In-fusible.	Vitreous.	Transparent.
GARNET, . . GROSSULARIA, ALMANDINE, .	Varied colour, . . Tint most esteemed, violet red, . . .	Silica, ... 40·00 Alumina, . . . 20·00 Oxide of iron, . . 34·00 Lime, ... 4·00 (*See page* 173).	Cubic System.	3·65 to 4·22	6·5 to 7·5	Simple.	1·76	0·033	same.	Fusible before the blow-pipe.	Vitreous and slightly resinous.	Varying from transparent to opaque.

GENERAL CHARACTERISTICS OF PRECIOUS STONES—(*Continued*).

NAME.	COLOUR.	COMPOSITION.	System of Crystallization.	Specific Gravity.	Place in the Scale of Hardness.	Refraction.	Index of Refraction.	Dispersive Power.	Electrical Properties.	Fusibility.	Lustre.	Transparency.
HYACINTH, . ZIRCON, . .	Brownish red, . . Colourless, yellow, greenish, . . .	Zircona, ... 66·00 Silica, ... 34·00 Oxide of iron, . traces.	Prismatic.	4·47	7·5	Double to a high degree.	1·99	0·044	Is electric by friction.	In-fusible.	Vitreous Resinous.	Transparent.
JADE, . . .	Pale green, and olive coloured, . . .	Silica, ... 58·00 Lime, ... 13·00 Magnesia, . . . 25·00 Oxide of iron, . . 2·00 Alumina, . . . 3·00	Not Crystallized.	2·97	,,	,,	,,	,,	same.	Fusible.	Milky white.	Semi-transparent.
TOURMALINE,	Showing all the colours from the hyaline aspect, nearly pure, to an opacity the most complete.	Boric acid, . . . 7·00 Silica, ... 41·00 Alumina, . . . 40·00 Oxide of iron and manganese, . . 6·00 Alkaline base, . . 5·00	Rhomboidal.	3·07	8	Double.	1·62	0·028	Taking electricity by friction and by heat.	Fusible.	Vitreous.	Transparent to opaque.
LABRADORITE,	Different colours, upon gray ground,	Silica, ... 55·00 Alumina, . . . 28·00 Lime, ... 12·00 Soda, ... 5·00	Prismatic.	2·5 to 2·7		Double.					Vitreous.	Opaline.
TURQUOISE, .	Pale blue and greenish blue, . . .	Alumina, . . . 44·50 Phosphoric acid, . 30·90 Oxide of copper, . 4·00 ,, iron, . . 1·50 Water, ... 19·00	,,	2·83 to 3	6	,,	,,	,,	none.	In-fusible.	Vitreous.	Semi-transparent.
		Silica, . . . 49·00 Alumina, . . . 11·00										

www.ingramcontent.com/pod-product-compliance
Lightning Source LLC
LaVergne TN
LVHW010212110826
845151LV00004B/1067